A Little Book of

Quotes from Karl Marx

Simon Blackburn

Proletarius Books

Published by **Proletarius Books**

Copyright © Simon Blackburn, 2016

The moral right of the author has been asserted.

First Published 2016

Visit: www.proletariusbooks.com

ISBN 978-0-9935242-0-2

Introduced, Translated and Edited by

Simon Blackburn

Forthcoming by Simon Blackburn

The Communist Manifesto: The Definitive Edition (2016)

Marxist Political Strategy (2016)

An Interview with Karl Marx (2016)

Filth Society (2017)

Contents

Acknowledgements

I never intended to put together, let alone have published, this book. I've spent the best part of the last six to seven years working simultaneously on three other books (concerned with developing a critique of contemporary capitalist society and, in particular, an examination of the nature of social order and the meaning of crime), and I now find myself nearing completion of these works. I've laboured on these books as an 'independent scholar' (not attached to a university), and being without a regular or full-time income has made things difficult. So I've had to rely on the support of a great many people – family and friends. *They know who they are, and I thank them*. I wish to have it acknowledged that the British State – its so-called 'welfare' arm – has *not* supported (or in any way financially assisted) me during these hard years. Indeed, its local government has made life – for myself and my family – unnecessarily oppressive (such is the moronic attitude of mindless, spiteful bureaucrats). As far as the State is concerned, I've been left to rot … but that's a story for another time. Nonetheless, I believe acknowledgement ought to be made of both those who provide support and those who fail to do so.

I now find myself nearing completion of the three books I've been working on and, in the process of undertaking research on these projects, I have gathered an immense collection of notes and quotes connected to the various sources that I have drawn upon. This is especially the case as regards my engagement with the texts of 'classic Marxism'. And so, on looking through my notebooks, I found that I was readily able to assemble the material at hand to produce *three additional* book-length studies: one on Marxist politics, another on Marx's thought generally, as well as this – a short book dedicated to nothing but out-of-context quotes from Marx and Engels. And so, as I finalise for publication the three 'proper' books that I have spent years working on, I have also put together three 'supplementary' publications. This one, the least substantial of them all, is the first to be published. Whether you agree or disagree with the ideas of Marx and Engels, I think you'll find they said some amazing things!

Introduction

This tiny book presents over 100 pages of quotes – some short, others long – from the works of Karl Marx and Frederick Engels. Their combined body of writing has been, and continues to be, highly influential; on the one hand, it has substantially contributed to the development of modern social science and our understanding of society,[1] and, on the other, their revolutionary ideas have been interpreted and acted upon in a myriad of ways that have shaped the formation of the modern world.[2] Notwithstanding the title of this book (which refers solely to Marx), the writings of both men are sourced herein. Throughout the last century and a half, Marx and Engels have – sometimes rightly and *all too often* wrongly – been assigned by commentators a variety of opinions and perspectives, and unfortunately both men have often been *mis*quoted. Here, care and attention has been made to correctly present quotations from their work.

---

[1] See S. Blackburn "Social Science: In Retrospect and Prospect", *The Graduate Journal of Social Science*, Vol 1, Issue 1, pp. 167-88, 2004

[2] For readers interested in the political-strategic revolutionary ideas of Marx and Engels, and how such ideas were interpreted by certain subsequent Marxists of the 'classic' period (up to 1922), see my *Marxist Political Strategy* (2016).

To offer the reader a brief biographical overview,[3] Karl Marx and Frederick Engels met in Paris in 1844, forming a strong friendship that would last until Marx's death in 1883. Throughout their adult lives the two friends set forth a joint body of work that, on the one hand, aimed at developing a critique of capitalism and, on the other, sought to advance a communist alternative. In the early years of their partnership, Marx and Engels collaborated on a number of works, including *The Holy Family* (1844), *The German Ideology* (1846), and *The Communist Manifesto* (1848). In subsequent years, though often separated, with Marx living in exile in London and Engels residing in Manchester, the two corresponded by letter on an almost daily basis, and each supported the other in the production of later publications. Throughout, it was Marx who constituted the more dominant creative thinker, as well as the more prodigious writer, and hence his name rightly defines their combined work.

Karl Marx was born in Prussia in 1818. Initially studying law, and later philosophy, at both Bonn and Berlin, Marx finally graduated with a PhD from the University of Jena, in 1841. Embarking on a career in journalism, in the early 1840's Marx came into contact with the embryonic socialist and communist ideas that where then popular in certain radical circles in France and Germany. Influenced by these, while simultaneously developing his understanding of economic theory, by 1844 Marx had begun to set forth his own conception of communism. Working jointly with Engels, the culmination of their 1845-6 efforts – namely, *The German Ideology* (published posthumously) – constitute an epistemological rupture from previous modes of social science thought, and represent their moment of arrival at the theory of historical materialism. For the first time, the proletariat was

---

[3] The following is adapted from my *Marxist Political Strategy* (2016).

identified as the only class capable of liberating humankind from the condition of societal fracture, with victory of the proletariat over the bourgeoisie singularly achievable through revolutionary political action.

Frederick Engels (1820–95) was likewise born in Prussia. As the elder son of an industrialist, in 1842 Engels was sent to work at the family textile-manufacturing firm in Manchester, England. Demonstrating an early interest in Hegelian philosophy, as well as a talent for radical literary and journalistic pursuits, Engels undertook a critical study on the state of degradation and impoverishment suffered by the proletariat in and around Manchester, presenting his findings as *The Conditions of the Working Class in England* (1845). The book concludes calling for proletarian emancipation by way of the formation of a political movement of the working class, with their salvation being the realisation of communism. Having establishing his friendship with Marx, Engels subsequently settled in Manchester in 1849, remaining there until 1870. Although intensely disliking his work in the family business, it provided Engels with a means to offer Marx a source of financial support. Engels moved to London in 1870, where he resided until his death.

Marx and Engels made their initial move into working class politics in 1846, joining the communist League of the Just (a tiny organisation, active in Germany, France and Britain). Previously, the League had been characterised by a utopian outlook, but under Marx and Engels' influence it was reoriented in-line with their theory of historical materialism. In late 1847, both men were tasked with drawing up a statement of principles for the League, for which they produced *The Communist Manifesto*. This polemic is the foundation of modern communism, boldly proclaiming the overthrow of the bourgeoisie by the proletariat and, with it, abolition of society based on class antagonisms, resulting in the formation of a new, classless society.

Following the demise of the revolutionary ethos of continental Europe in 1848, Marx and Engels withdrew from active political practice. Throughout much of the next decade and a half, Marx personally endured conditions of dire poverty as well as frequent yet spasmodic poor health. It was during this period that he spent much of his available time working as a journalist, as a European correspondent, writing articles for the *New York Daily Tribune*. He also endeavoured to continue his economic studies, accumulating several hundred pages of notes that eventually became known as *Grundrisse*. By the mid-1860's, Marx had drawn-up the bulk of the vast manuscript for the three volumes of *Capital*. Volume One was published in 1867, and this work represents his *magnum opus* – it is here that he develops a sustained and detailed critique of political economy, revealing the 'laws of motion' of the capitalist economic system, and exposing the contradictions inherent in its mode of production.

At this point in his life, Marx finally found himself in a position to financially support his family, and he once again sought to engage in the organisational activity of the proletarian movement. Marx joined the newly founded International Working Men's Association (or 'First' International), being elected in 1864 to its General Council, based in London. Taking a leading position, he drew up the International's *Inaugural Address* and *Provisional Rules*, which, although endued with Marx's theory of modern communism, are presented in a much more cautious and protracted style as compared to the *Manifesto*. Marx, together with Engels (who joined the General Council in 1870), worked vigorously to structure and organise the International in such ways that it might effectively pursue valuable reforms (e.g. the eight hour working day) through the existing constitutional framework of the capitalist State, and in the process both men hoped to transform the working class into a politicised movement capable of revolution.

At its peak, membership of the International, both individual and affiliated, reached over 2 million, and was especially active in many parts of Western Europe. In consequence, by the early 1870's questions about Marx and the International were being asked in the British Parliament, as well as in the leading national press, resulting in the British Government initiating an investigation into Marx's activities. Much of this notoriety reflected the revolutionary zeal of Marx's published analyses in relation to the Paris Commune (March-May 1871), when the working class of Paris briefly formed a government founded on socialist principles, before being crushed by reactionary forces. Marx's *The Civil War in France* (1871) described the Commune as the first genuine revolutionary attempt by the modern proletariat to seize control of political power; and Engels – in his 1891 Introduction to Marx's study – defined the democratic organisation of the Commune's Parisian working class as constituting the realisation of the 'dictatorship of the proletariat'. Being widely circulated, translated into numerous languages and published throughout Europe and in the USA, *The Civil War in France* is one of Marx's most influential political tracts.

Marx and Engels remained active in the International until 1872, when its General Council moved to New York (where it disbanded four years later). From then onwards, the direct involvement of the two men in working class political organisation tended to diminish; although they both continued to write on the subject of politics, as well as correspond with – and offer guidance to – the emerging leaders of the various social democratic parties that were established throughout most of Europe from the mid-1870's onwards. An important intervention in this regard was the *Critique of the Gotha Programme*, written by Marx in 1875, concerning the draft programme of the newly formed German Social Democratic Party. In the *Critique*, Marx offers his most detailed presentation of revolutionary strategy, as well as elucidating the principles of communism. The *Critique* is also notable for its analysis – albeit brief – on the nature and role of the capitalist State, understood as an organ superimposed upon society for the reproduction of social and political inequalities. For Marx, the transition to communism involves the abolition of these inequalities, and with them the abolition of the State itself, by way of self-liberation on the part of the working class through their conquest of political power. This subject was developed by Engels, both in *Socialism: Utopian and Scientific* (1880) and *Origin of the Family, Private Property and the State* (1884). Engels traces the broad history of the State, arguing that the ultimate seizure of political power by the working class will effectively result in the process of withering away of the State; for the working class, in attaining dominance in society, does away with all class distinctions: as there is no longer a subordinate class to oppress, so the State – a mechanism for the maintenance of class antagonisms – becomes superfluous.

Marx and Engels called for, and sought to develop, a politically organised revolutionary working class movement that would overthrow capitalism, abolish the existing State apparatus and substitute this with its own rule, in the form of a transitional socialist stage of society, eventually leading to the establishment of communism. The two men were vividly aware of the sad, terrible and soul-destroying way the immense majority of men and women are forced to spend their daily lives, and they developed in their early writings a critique of capitalist society based on humanistic criteria. In their mature work, the founders of Marxism advanced a scientific conception, criticising capitalism on the basis of its inherent structural contradictions. Put simply, both men viewed capitalism as possessing enormous capabilities: economically, politically and socially. This stage of society has, for example, created for humankind, for the first time in history, the possibility of providing a secure and decent life for every person. But by its very nature as a social formation characterised by systemic fracture, capitalism is incapable of realising this potential.

Communism is presented as the solution to these contradictions; it comes about as a result of social antagonisms, by the defeat of the bourgeoisie through the revolutionary political action of the working class. With the victory of the working class, the age of enslaving subordination and exploitation of human by human comes to a close. The transition to communism is considered as establishing an economy based on the satisfaction of needs, rather than a distribution of goods and services in accordance with the competitive ability to pay. Marx and Engels' communism, portrayed as a genuinely democratic mode of life involving universal participation in the determination of affairs, and characterised by the association of free and liberated individuals, assures the subsistence and enrichment of every human by virtue of being a member of society.

*

As a whole, the corpus of written work available by Marx and Engels is prodigious, consisting of some 50 large volumes (see their *Collected Works*, now available in English, published by Lawrence and Wishart). This immense body of writing covers a vast range of 'disciplinary' fields (as they now exist in university circles) – not simply economics and politics (or, more traditionally, 'political economy') but other areas such as sociology, criminology, social policy, psychology, philosophy, anthropology, history, even mathematics. And these writings often extend beyond such disciplines, to include juvenilia, poetry and love letters. The content thus shifts from the objectively scientific and theoretical to the highly personal. The quotes found in this book reflect this diversity of topics.

Please be aware, this book is not intended to educate; it is *not* a scholarly contribution to knowledge. Its purpose is merely to present a collection of quotations from a vast range of written sources, including letters, newspaper articles, journal papers, pamphlets, unpublished manuscripts, books, speeches, and so on. If you are interested in the thought of Marx and Engels, or classic Marxism more generally, then you may in turn find these quotes curious and thought-provoking. At best, many of these quotes are fun to read, and may assist elucidate some of the ideas associated with Marx and Engels. And if, having read a quote that piques ones fascination, the reader is inspired to look-up the full text by Marx and Engels then this book has fulfilled an important role. A select bibliography – of works by Marx and Engels – is included towards the end of the book.

The quotes are presented in British English (so, for example, it's 'labour' not 'labor'). They are offered in no particular order (neither chronological, nor by way of some perceived order of importance). Certainly not everything that *could* be quoted from Marx or Engels is included – so this book serves only to whet ones appetite! Note, I provide details of the source from which each quote is taken, and state the year it was originally written (and, where it differs, I also cite the year of first publication).

I am responsible for the selections made, as well as the translation and presentation of these 362 quotes. For any inaccuracies, my apologies.

A Note on Translation

All the quotes contained herein are drawn from texts written between 1837 and 1895. Many of the most important works by Marx and Engels were first published during their lifetimes. For those texts published in English during this period, I have relied on those editions here. Much of the material that had remained hitherto unpublished finally became available in-print during the years immediately following Engels' death – such as Marx's article 'Value, Price and Profit' which, although written in 1865, was not first published until 1898 (by Marx's daughter Eleanor). Again, I have relied on these early translations.

Marx and Engels typically wrote in German – although not always doing so; for instance, Marx wrote *The Poverty of Philosophy* (1847) in French. Many of their writings were translated to English during their lifetimes (e.g. Engels' *Condition of the Working Class in England* was published in German in 1845, and first appeared in English in 1887). Available English translations do, on occasion, differ remarkably as regards many textual particulars. For instance, the first English edition of the *Manifesto* – as appeared in late 1850, in *The Red Republican* (edited by G. Julian Harney), translated by Helen Macfarlane – differs in a number of instances from later translations.[4] To offer a couple of examples: This 1850 edition starts with "A frightful hobgoblin

---

[4] See *The Communist Manifesto: Definitive Edition* (2016), in which I discuss such differences.

stalks throughout Europe. We are haunted by a ghost, the ghost of Communism." It goes on to say, "Hitherto the history of Society has been the history of the battles between the classes composing it." The English edition of 1888, translated by Samuel Moore (in cooperation with Frederick Engels), presents these sentences as "A spectre is haunting Europe – the spectre of Communism" and "The history of all hitherto existing society is the history of class struggles." We are, today, most familiar with these later translations. Nonetheless both versions are legitimate.

Some readers may identify specific quotes presented in this book that do not precisely accord with known translations. This is because, in seeking to *interpret* what Marx or Engels were saying – in those manuscripts that went unpublished during their own lifetimes – so I have, where necessary, offered a *changed* translation (as compared to existing publications). Typically, such changes are relatively minor and do not alter the meaning of the quoted passage – to illustrate: "Life is not determined by consciousness, but consciousness by life" is the standard translation of this sentence[5] from *The German Ideology*. Yet, on re-visiting the original German version, I find this sentence to be more exactly translated as "It is not consciousness that determines life, but life determines consciousness." On the occasion that I present an interpretation of a passage that does significantly differ in meaning from previous versions, I duly inform the reader.

Of course, I do not claim to have offered 'better' translations than anyone else – and I certainly direct the reader to existing publications.

---

[5] The sentence, in the German original, reads: "Nicht das Bewußtsein bestimmt das Leben, sondern das Leben bestimmt das Bewußtsein."

Quotes

Every beginning is difficult, holds in all sciences.

Marx, 'Preface' to the first German edition of *Capital, Vol. I* (1867)

Communism … is the solution to the riddle of history and knows itself to be the solution.

Marx, 'Economic and Philosophic Manuscripts' (1844; first published 1932)

Hitherto people have always made up for themselves false conceptions about themselves, about what they are and what they ought to be. They have arranged their relationships according to their ideas of God, of normal man, and so on. The figments of their brains have got out of their hands. They, the creators, have bowed before their creations. We liberate them from the chimeras, the ideas, dogmas, imaginary beings under whose yoke they wither. We rebel against the reign of thoughts.

Marx & Engels, 'German Ideology' (1845-6; first published 1932)

If you love without evoking love in return – if through the vital expression of yourself as a loving person you fail to become a loved person, then your love is impotent, it is a misfortune.

Marx, 'Economic and Philosophic Manuscripts' (1844; first published 1932)

Ignorance has never yet helped anyone!

Marx, at a meeting in Brussels (in response to Weitling) (1846; unknown first publication)

The conditions from which we begin are not arbitrary, not dogmas, but real premises from which one can abstract only in the imagination. They are the real individuals, their activity and their material conditions, both those which they find already present and those generated by their activity. These premises are verifiable in a purely empirical way.

Marx & Engels, 'German Ideology' (1845-6; first published 1932)

Religious suffering is at one and the same time the *expression* of real suffering and a *protest* against real suffering. Religion is the sigh of the oppressed creature, the heart of a heartless world, and it is the soul of soulless conditions. It is the *opium* of the people.

Marx, 'Critique of Hegel's *Philosophy of Right*. Introduction.' (1844)

Reason has always existed, but not always in a reasonable form.

Marx, 'Letter to Ruge' (1843; first published 1844)

A few days in my old man's factory have sufficed to bring me face to face with this beastliness, which I had rather overlooked ... it is impossible to carry on communist propaganda on a large scale and at the same time engage in huckstering and industry.

Engels, 'Letter to Marx' (1845; first published 1913)

The first premise of all human history is, of course, the existence of living human individuals.

Marx & Engels, 'German Ideology' (1845-6; first published 1932)

Under the system of private property ... Each tries to establish over the other an alien power, in the hope of thereby achieving satisfaction of his own selfish needs.

Marx, 'Economic and Philosophic Manuscripts' (1844; first published 1932)

But, if constructing the future and settling everything for all times are not our affair, it is all the more clear what we have to accomplish at present: I am referring to *ruthless criticism of all that exists*, ruthless both in the sense of not being afraid of the results it arrives at and in the sense of being just as little afraid of conflict with the powers that be.

Marx, 'Letter to Ruge' (1843; first published 1844)

...the whole of history is nothing but a continual transformation of human nature.

Marx, 'Poverty of Philosophy' (1847)

...in general there remain only two classes in the population – the working class and the capitalist class.

Marx, 'Economic and Philosophic Manuscripts' (1844; first published 1932)

To formulate a question is to answer it.

Marx, 'On the Jewish Question' (1843; first published 1844)

Since the essence of *man* is the *true community* of man, men, by activating their own essence, produce, create this human community, this social being which is no abstract, universal power standing over the solitary individual, but is the essence of every individual, his own activity, his own life, his own spirit, his own wealth. Therefore, this *true community* does not come into being as the product of reflection but it arises out of the *need* and the *egoism* of individuals, i.e. it arises directly from their own activity.

Marx, 'Excerpts from James Mill's *Elements of Political Economy*' (1844; first published 1932)

Capital is *stored-up labour*.

Marx, 'Economic and Philosophic Manuscripts' (1844; first published 1932)

…political emancipation is not the complete and consistent form of *human* emancipation.

The limitations of political emancipation are immediately evident from the fact that the *state* can liberate itself from a restriction without man himself being *truly* free of it, that a state can be a *free state* without man himself being *a free man*.

Marx, 'On the Jewish Question' (1843; first published 1844)

Political Economy regards the proletarian ... like a horse, he must receive enough to enable him to work. It does not consider him, during the time when he is not working, as a human being.

Marx, 'Economic and Philosophic Manuscripts' (1844; first published 1932)

It is not consciousness that determines life, but life determines consciousness.

Marx & Engels, 'German Ideology' (1845-6; first published 1932)

Forgive dear father, the illegible script and the poor style; it is nearly 4 in the morning, the candle is completely burnt out and the eyes dim; a true unrest has taken mastery of me and I will not be able to calm the excited spirits until I am in your dear presence. Please give my greetings to my sweet, dear Jenny. Her letter has already been read twelve times through, and I always discover new delights. It is in every respect, including style, the most beautiful letter that I can imagine from a woman.

Marx, 'Letter to His Father' (1837; first published 1897)

Bring paper money into a country where this use of paper is unknown, and everyone will laugh at your subjective imagination.

Marx, 'Doctoral Thesis' (1841; first published 1902)

We develop new principles for the world out of the world's own principles. We do not say to the world: Cease your struggles, they are foolish; we will give you the true slogan of struggle. We merely show the world what it is really fighting for, and consciousness is something that it *has to* acquire, even if it does not want to.

Marx, 'Letter to Ruge' (1843; first published 1844)

Political economy came into being as a natural result of the expansion of trade, and with its appearance elementary, unscientific huckstering was replaced by a developed system of licensed fraud, an entire science of enrichment.

Engels, 'Outlines of a Critique Political Economy' (1844)

But man is no abstract being sitting outside the world. Man is the world of man, state, society. This state, this society, produce religion, which is an *inverted consciousness of the world*, because they are an *inverted world*. Religion is the general theory of this world, its encyclopaedic compendium, its logic in popular form, its spiritual *point d'honneur*, its enthusiasm, its moral sanction, its solemn complement, and its universal basis of consolation and justification. It is the *fantastic realisation* of the human essence because the human essence has not acquired any true reality. The struggle against religion is therefore indirectly the struggle against *that world* whose spiritual *aroma* is religion.

Marx, 'Critique of Hegel's *Philosophy of Right*. Introduction.' (1844)

Only when real, individual man resumes the abstract citizen into himself and as an individual man has become a *species-being* in his empirical life, his individual work and his individual relationships, only when man has recognised and organised his *own forces* as *social forces* so that social force is no longer separated from him in the form of *political* force, only then will human emancipation be completed.

Marx, 'On the Jewish Question' (1843; first published 1844)

In the economic system, under the rule of private property, the interest which any individual has in society is in inverse proportion to the interest which society has in him…

Marx, 'Economic and Philosophic Manuscripts' (1844; first published 1932)

How individuals express their life, so they are. What they are, therefore, coincides with their production, with what they produce, as well as how they produce. The nature of individuals thus depends on the material conditions of their production.

Marx & Engels, 'German Ideology' (1845-6; first published 1932)

The *social* reality of nature and *human* natural science or the *natural science of man* are identical expressions.

Marx, 'Economic and Philosophic Manuscripts' (1844; first published 1932)

If we have chosen the position in life in which we can most of all work for mankind, no burdens can bow us down, because they are sacrifices for the benefit of all; then we shall experience no petty, limited, selfish joy, but our happiness will belong to millions, our deeds will live on quietly but perpetually at work, and over our ashes will be shed the hot tears of noble people.

Marx, 'Letter to His Father' (1837; first published 1897)

In the framework of private property my individuality has been alienated to the point where I loathe this [labour] activity, it is torture for me. It is in fact no more than the *appearance* of activity and for that reason it is only a *forced* labour imposed on me *not* through an *inner necessity* but through an *external* arbitrary need.

Marx, 'Excerpts from James Mill's *Elements of Political Economy*' (1844; first published 1932)

History calls those men the greatest who have ennobled themselves by working for the common good; experience acclaims as happiest the man who has made the greatest number of people happy.

Marx, 'Letter to His Father' (1837; first published 1897)

But an end which requires unjustified means is no justifiable end.

Marx, 'On the Freedom of the Press' (1842)

The worker places his life in the object; but it no longer belongs to him, but to the object. The greater his activity, therefore, the fewer objects the worker possesses. What the product of his labour is, he is not. Therefore, the greater this product, the less he is himself.

Marx, 'Economic and Philosophic Manuscripts' (1844; first published 1932)

Only in the name of the general rights of society can a particular class vindicate its general rule.

Marx, 'Critique of Hegel's *Philosophy of Right.* Introduction.' (1844)

As Prometheus, having stolen fire from heaven, begins to build houses and to settle upon the earth, so philosophy, expanded to be the whole world, turns against the world of appearance. The same now with the philosophy of Hegel.

Marx, 'Notebooks on Epicurean Philosophy' (1839; first published 1927)

History has been resolved into superstition for long enough. We are now resolving superstition into history.

Marx, 'On the Jewish Question' (1843; first published 1844)

Greek philosophy seems to have met with something with which a good tragedy is not supposed to meet, namely, a dull ending.

Marx, 'Doctoral Thesis' (1841; first published 1901)

Consciousness is ... from the outset a social product and remains so as long as people exist at all.

Marx & Engels, 'German Ideology' (1845-6; first published 1932)

The State in its own way abolishes distinctions based on *birth, rank, education* and *occupation* when it declares birth, rank, education and occupation to be *non-political* distinctions...

Marx, 'On the Jewish Question' (1843; first published 1844)

What is genuine is proved in the fire, what is false we shall not miss in our ranks. The opponents must grant us that youth has never before flocked to our colours in such numbers ... in the end, one will be found among us who will prove that the sword of enthusiasm is just as good as the sword of genius.

Engels, 'Anti-Schelling' (1841; first published 1842)

...'atheism' ... reminds one of children, assuring everyone who is ready to listen to them that they are not afraid of the bogy man.

Marx, 'Letter to Ruge' (1842; first published in 1844)

What is the worldly cult of the Jew? *Haggling*. What is his worldly God? *Money*.

Marx, 'On the Jewish Question' (1843; first published 1844)

Thus, the *revolution of a people* and the *emancipation of a particular class* of bourgeois society coincide, so that *a* class stands for the whole of society, conversely all the defects of society are concentrated in another class, this particular class must be the class which gives general contention, the incorporation of a general barrier; this requires one particular sphere of society to appear as the *notorious crime* of the whole of society, so that the liberation of this sphere appears as universal self-liberation.

Marx, 'Critique of Hegel's *Philosophy of Right*. Introduction.' (1844)

...the misery of the worker is in inverse proportion to the power and volume of his production...

Marx, 'Economic and Philosophic Manuscripts' (1844; first published 1932)

The tendency to give rise to the *world market* is directly given in the concept of capital itself.

Marx, 'Grundrisse' (1857; first published 1939)

Consciousness can never be anything else than conscious existence, and the existence of people is their real life-process.

Marx & Engels, 'German Ideology' (1845-6; first published 1932)

A spectre is haunting Europe – the spectre of communism.

Marx & Engels, 'Communist Manifesto' (1848)

In the formation of a class with *radical chains*, a class of civil society which is not a class of civil society, a class which is the dissolution of all classes, a sphere which has a universal character because of its universal suffering and which lays claim to no *particular right* because the wrong it suffers is not a *particular wrong*, but is *absolute injustice*, which can no longer claim a *historical* title, but merely a *human* one ... and finally a sphere which cannot emancipate itself without emancipating itself from all the other spheres of society – and thus emancipating all the other spheres of society; which is, in a word, the *complete loss* of humanity, so only through the *complete recovery of humanity* can this class itself win. This dissolution of society as a particular class is the *proletariat*.

Marx, 'Critique of Hegel's *Philosophy of Right*. Introduction.' (1844)

The ideas of the ruling class are in every epoch the ruling ideas, i.e. the class which is the ruling material force of society, is at the same time its ruling intellectual force. The class which has the means of material production at its disposal, has control at the same time over the means of mental production, in order that, at the same time, the ideas of those who lack the means of mental production are subject to it. The ruling ideas are nothing more than the ideal expression of the dominant material relationships, the prevailing material conditions followed as thoughts; consequent of the conditions which make a class the ruling one, therefore, the rule of their ideas.

Marx & Engels, 'German Ideology' (1845-6; first published 1932)

The State is based on this contradiction. It is based on the contradiction between public and private life, between general and particular interests. For this reason, the State must confine itself to formal, negative activities...

Marx, 'Critical Notes on the Article "The King of Prussia and Social Reform." By a Prussian.' (1844)

The bourgeoisie is just as necessary a precondition for the socialist revolution as is the proletariat itself.

Engels, 'On Social Relations in Russia' (1874; first published 1875)

But the struggle between class and class is a political struggle.

Marx, 'Poverty of Philosophy' (1847)

...we must start by noting the first condition of all human existence, and therefore, of all history, namely the requirement that people must be in a position to live, to "make history". But life involves before all else eating and drinking, habitation, clothing and many other things. The first historical act is thus the production of the means to satisfy these needs, the production of material life itself, and indeed this is an historical act, a fundamental condition of all history, which today, as thousands of years ago, must be met daily and hourly, to sustain human life.

Marx & Engels, 'German Ideology' (1845-6; first published 1932)

The weapon of criticism cannot replace the criticism of weapons, material force must be overthrown by material force…

Marx, 'Critique of Hegel's *Philosophy of Right*. Introduction.' (1844)

Capital is … the *power to command* labour and its products. The capitalist possesses this power not on account of his personal or human properties but in so far as he is an *owner* of capital.

Marx, 'Economic and Philosophic Manuscripts' (1844; first published 1932)

The relations of production in their totality constitute what are called *the social relations, society*, and, specifically, a society at *a definite stage of historical development*, a society with a peculiar, distinctive character. Ancient society, feudal society, bourgeois society are such totalities of production relations, each of which at the same time denotes a special stage of development in the history of mankind.

Marx, 'Wage Labour and Capital' (1847; first published 1849)

Capital is not a simple relation, but a *process*…

Marx, 'Grundrisse' (1857; first published 1939)

…it is the ultimate aim of this work, to lay bare the economic law of motion of modern society…

Marx, 'Preface' to the first German edition of *Capital, Vol. I* (1867)

...the object that labour produces, its product, stands opposed to it as *something alien*, as a *power independent* of the producer. The product of labour is labour embodied and made material in an object, it is the *objectification* of labour. The realisation of labour is its objectification. In the sphere of political economy this realisation of labour appears as a *loss of reality* for the worker, objectification as *loss and bondage to the object*, and appropriation as *estrangement*, as *alienation*.

Marx, 'Economic and Philosophic Manuscripts' (1844; first published 1932)

The question whether objective truth can be attributed to human thinking is not a question of theory but is a *practical* question.

Marx, 'Theses on Feuerbach: Thesis II' (1845; first published 1888)

The worker becomes poorer the more wealth he produces, the more his production increases in power and extent. The worker becomes an ever cheaper commodity the more commodities he produces. The *devaluation* of the human world grows in direct proportion to the *increase in value* of the world of things.

Marx, 'Economic and Philosophic Manuscripts' (1844; first published 1932)

History is the judge — its executioner, the proletarian.

Marx, 'Speech at Anniversary of *The People's Paper*' (1856)

Wages are determined by the fierce struggle between capitalist and worker. The capitalist is inevitably victorious. The capitalist can live longer without the worker than the worker can without him.

Marx, 'Economic and Philosophic Manuscripts' (1844; first published 1932)

One can distinguish man from animals by consciousness, by religion, by anything else you like. They themselves being to distinguish themselves from animals as soon as they begin to *produce* their means of subsistence, a step which is conditioned by their physical organisation.

Marx & Engels, 'German Ideology' (1845-6; first published 1932)

[Francis] Bacon says really important people have so many relations to nature and the world, so many objects of interest, that they easily get over any loss. I am not one of those important people. My child's death has affected me so greatly that I feel the loss as bitterly as on the first day.

Marx, 'Letter to Lasalle' (1855 – written some 3 months after the death of his infant son Edgar; unknown first publication)

For wages, the lowest and the only required rate is that necessary for the subsistence of the worker during work and enough extra to support a family and prevent the race of workers from dying out.

Marx, 'Economic and Philosophic Manuscripts' (1844; first published 1932)

The human being is in the most literal sense a *governmental animal*, not merely a gregarious animal, but an animal which can individuate itself only in the midst of society.[6] Production by an isolated individual outside society ... is as much of an absurdity as is the development of language without individuals living *together* and talking to each other.

Marx, 'Grundrisse' (1857; first published 1939)

The essential condition of the emancipation of the working class is the abolition of all classes ...

Marx, 'Poverty of Philosophy' (1847)

---

[6] With regard to a particular phrase here, I have notably differed from existing interpretation. In *Grundrisse*, Marx says "The human being is in the most literal sense a ζῶον πολιτιχόν, not merely a gregarious animal, but an animal which can individuate itself only in the midst of society." The phrase ζῶον πολιτιχόν is problematic. It is Greek, and directly translates to *animal policies*. Existing translations present this phrase as 'political animal'. But I tend to think that Marx meant something else (especially as he typically associated 'political' with class-divided social formations only, not society generally). Marx uses the phrase on a second occasion in *Grundrisse*, saying "But human beings become individuals only through the historical process. Man appears originally as a *species-being, clan being, herd animal* – although in no way whatever as a ζῶον πολιτιχόν in the political sense." If ζῶον πολιτιχόν translates to 'political animal' then this latter use of the phrase makes the sentence read: "...although in no way whatever as a political animal in the political sense." This translation becomes rather nonsensical. What purpose does it serve to designate man as not 'political' in the 'political sense'? I prefer to interpret the term πολιτιχόν not literally as 'policy' but as 'governmental' (denoting governance, administration and organisation, not politics).

The production of life … appears as twofold – on the one hand as a natural, on the other hand as a social relation. Understanding social in the sense of the cooperation of several individuals, no matter under what conditions, in what manner and for what purpose.

Marx & Engels, 'German Ideology' (1845-6; first published 1932)

If the proletariat during its contest with the bourgeoisie is compelled, by the force of circumstances, to organise itself as a class, if, by means of revolution, it makes itself the ruling class, and, as such, sweeps away by force the old conditions of production, then it will, along with these conditions, have swept away the conditions for the existence of class antagonisms and of classes generally, and will thereby have abolished its own supremacy as a class.

Marx & Engels, 'Communist Manifesto' (1848)

Such belletristic phrases, which connect everything to everything else by way of some analogy, may even appear insightful the first time they are expressed, all the more so if they identify the most unrelated things. Repeated, however, and then repeated with outright complacency as statements of scientific worth, they are entirely and essentially ridiculous. Good only for belletristic sophomores and empty chatterboxes who defile all the sciences with their liquorice-sweet filth.

Marx, 'Grundrisse' (1857; first published 1939)

As ... the competition among capitalists increases, there is a growing concentration of capital, the big capitalists ruin the small ones and a section of the former capitalists sinks into the class of the workers...

Marx, 'Economic and Philosophic Manuscripts' (1844; first published 1932)

At a certain stage of development, the material productive forces of society come into conflict with the existing relations of production or – this merely expresses the same thing in legal terms – with the property relations within the framework of which they have operated hitherto. From forms of development of the productive forces these relations turn into their fetters. Then begins an era of social revolution. The changes in the economic foundation lead sooner or later to the transformation of the whole immense superstructure.

Marx, 'Preface' to *A Contribution to the Critique of Political Economy* (1859)

Labour is, in the first place, a process in which both man and Nature participate, and in which man of his own accord starts, regulates, and controls the material re-actions between himself and Nature. He opposes himself to Nature as one of her own forces ... By thus acting on the external world and changing it, he at the same time changes his own nature.

Marx, 'Capital, Volume I' (1867)

A commodity has *a value*, because it is a *crystallisation of social labour*. The *greatness* of its value, or its *relative* value, depends upon the greater or less amount of that social substance contained in it; that is to say, on the relative mass of labour necessary for its production. The *relative values of commodities* are, therefore, determined by the *respective quantities* or *amounts of labour, worked up, realised, fixed in them*. The *correlative* quantities of commodities which can be produced in the *same time of labour* are *equal*. Or the value of one commodity is to the value of another commodity as the quantity of labour fixed in the one is the quantity of labour fixed in the other.

Marx, 'Value, Price and Profit' (1865; first published 1898)

The whole Darwinian theory of the struggle for existence is simply the transference from society to animate nature of Hobbes' theory of the war of every man against every man and the bourgeois economic theory of competition, along with the Malthusian theory of population … the same theories are next transferred back again from organic nature to history and their validity as eternal laws of human society announced to have been proved.

Engels, 'Letter to Lavrov' (1875; first published 1936)

Natural science will eventually incorporate into itself the science of man, just as the science of man will incorporate into itself natural science: there will be *one* science.

Marx, 'Economic and Philosophic Manuscripts' (1844; first published 1932)

It is altogether self-evident that, to be able to fight at all, the working class must organise itself domestically *as a class* and that its own country is the immediate arena of its struggle — insofar as its class struggle is national, not in substance, but, as the *Communist Manifesto* says, 'in form'.

Marx, 'Critique of the Gotha Programme' (1875; first published 1891)

The people are the producers of their conceptions, ideas, etc. – real, active people as they are conditioned by a definite development of their productive forces and the corresponding social intercourse, up to its furthest forms.

Marx & Engels, 'German Ideology' (1845-6; first published 1932)

Neither of us cares a straw for popularity. Let me cite one proof of this: such was my aversion to the personality cult that at the time of the International, when plagued by numerous moves – originating from various countries – to accord me public honour, I never allowed one of these to enter the domain of publicity, nor did I ever reply to them, save with an occasional snub. When Engels and I first joined the secret communist society, we did so only on condition that anything conducive to a superstitious belief in authority be eliminated from the Rules.

Marx, 'Letter to Blos' (1877; first published 1908)

Capital by its nature drives beyond every spatial barrier.

Marx, 'Grundrisse' (1857; first published 1939)

A philosopher produces ideas, a poet poems, a clergyman sermons, a professor compendia and so on. A criminal produces crimes. If we look a little closer at the connection between this latter branch of production and society as a whole, we shall rid ourselves of many prejudices. The criminal produces not only crimes but also criminal law, and with this also the professor who gives lectures on criminal law and in addition to this the inevitable compendium in which this same professor throws his lectures onto the general market as 'commodities' ... The criminal moreover produces the whole of the police and of criminal justice, constables, judges, hangmen, juries, etc.; and all these different lines of business, which form equally many categories of the social division of labour, develop different capacities of the human spirit, create new needs and new ways of satisfying them.

Marx, 'Theories of Surplus Value, Book One' (1861; first published 1905-10)

The morality of political economy is *gain*, labour and thrift, sobriety – and yet political economy promises to satisfy my needs.

Marx, 'Economic and Philosophic Manuscripts' (1844; first published 1932)

The moment you are absent, my love for you shows itself to be what it is, a giant, in which are crowded together all the energy of my spirit and all the character of my heart.

Marx, 'Love letter to his wife Jenny' (1865; unknown first publication)

[Bourgeois] society is invariably and inevitably opposed to the interest of the worker.

Marx, 'Economic and Philosophic Manuscripts' (1844; first published 1932)

The wealth of those societies in which the capitalist mode of production prevails, presents itself as "an immense accumulation of commodities," its unit being a single commodity. Our investigation must therefore begin with the analysis of a commodity.

Marx, 'Capital, Volume I' (1867)

The essential difference between human and animal society is that animals are at most *gatherers* whilst men are *producers*. This single but cardinal distinction alone makes it impossible simply to transfer the laws of animal societies to human societies ... At a certain stage, therefore, human production reaches a level where not only essential necessities but also luxuries are produced, even if, for the time being, they are only produced for a minority. Hence the struggle for existence – if we allow this category as valid here for a moment – transforms itself into a struggle for enjoyments, a struggle no longer for the mere means of *existence* but for the means of *development, socially produced* means of development, and at this stage the categories of the animal kingdom are no longer applicable.

Engels, 'Letter to Lavrov' (1875; first published 1936)

Doubt everything.

Marx, his favourite motto (during "Confessions" with relatives), (1865; unknown first publication)

Since the State is the form in which the individuals of a ruling class assert their common interests and in which the whole of bourgeois society of an epoch epitomises itself, it follows that all common institutions are mediated by the State, receiving a political form.

Marx & Engels, 'German Ideology' (1845-6; first published 1932)

In a future society, where the antagonism of classes will have ceased, where there will no longer be classes, use will no longer be determined by the *minimum* time of production; but the time of social production which will be devoted to the various objects will be determined by their degree of social utility.

Marx, 'Poverty of Philosophy' (1847)

The social relation of individuals to one another as a power over the individuals which has become autonomous, whether conceived as a force of nature, as happenstance or in whatever other form, is a necessary outcome of the fact that the point of departure is not the free social individual.

Marx, 'Grundrisse' (1857; first published 1939)

The bourgeoisie has through its exploitation of the world market given a cosmopolitan character to production and consumption in every country.

Marx & Engels, 'Communist Manifesto' (1848)

There is only one antidote to mental suffering, and that is physical pain.

Marx, 'Herr Vogt' (1860)

You would be altogether mistaken in fancying that the value of labour or any other commodity whatever is ultimately fixed by supply and demand. Supply and demand regulate nothing but the temporary *fluctuations* of market prices. They will explain to you why the market price of a commodity rises above or sinks below its *value*, but they can never account for that *value* itself.

Marx, 'Value, Price and Profit' (1865; first published 1898)

Workers of all countries, unite!

Marx, 'Inaugural Address of the [First] International' (1864)

The essential difference between the various economic forms of society, between, for instance, a society based on slave-labour, and one based on wage-labour, lies only in the mode in which this surplus-labour is in each case extracted from the actual producer, the labourer.

Marx, 'Capital, Volume I' (1867)

No social formation is ever destroyed before all the productive forces for which it is sufficient have been developed, and new superior relations of production never replace older ones before the material conditions for their existence have matured within the framework of the old society. Mankind thus inevitably sets itself only such tasks as it is able to solve, since closer examination will always show that the problem itself arises only when the material conditions for its solution are already present or at least in the course of formation.

Marx, 'Preface' to *A Contribution to the Critique of Political Economy* (1859)

Communism is the *positive* supersession of *private property* as *human self-estrangement*, and hence the true *appropriation* of the *human* essence through and for man; it is the complete restoration of man to himself as a *social*, i.e. human, being...

Marx, 'Economic and Philosophic Manuscripts' (1844; first published 1932)

Communism is for us not a *State*, which is to be established, an ideal to which reality [will] have to comply. We call communism the *real* movement which abolishes the present state of things. The conditions of this movement result from the premises now existing.

Marx & Engels, 'German Ideology' (1845-6; first published 1932)

Communism is the act of positing as the negation of the negation, and is therefore a *real* phase, necessary for the next period of historical development, in the emancipation and recovery of humankind.

Marx, 'Economic and Philosophic Manuscripts' (1844; first published 1932)

In a higher phase of communist society, after the enslaving subordination of the individual to the division of labour, and thereby also the antithesis between mental and physical labour, has vanished, after labour has become not only a means of life but life's prime want; after the productive forces have also increased with the all-round development of the individual, and all the springs of common wealth flow more abundantly – only then then can the narrow horizon of bourgeois right be crossed in its entirety and society inscribe on its banners: *From each according to his ability, to each according to his needs!*

Marx, 'Critique of the Gotha Programme' (1875; first published 1891)

One thing, however, is clear – Nature does not produce on the one side owners of money or commodities, and on the other men possessing nothing but their own labour-power. This relation has no natural basis, neither is its social basis one that is common to all historical periods. It is clearly the result of a past historical development, the product of many economic revolutions, of the extinction of a whole series of older forms of social production.

Marx, 'Capital, Volume I' (1867)

... [the] contradiction between the interest of the individual and of the community takes the form of the common interest as an independent *State*, separate from the real interests of individual and community, and at the same time as an illusory communality ... It follows that all struggles within the State, the struggle between democracy, aristocracy and monarchy, the struggle for the right to vote, etc., etc., are nothing but the illusory forms in which the real struggles of the different classes are fought out among each other ... and further, that each class which is striving for mastery, even when its domination, as is the case with the proletariat, postulates the abolition of the entire old form of society and of domination itself, first must conquer for itself political power representing their interest again as the general, which it is compelled at first to do.

Marx & Engels, 'German Ideology' (1845-6; first published 1932)

In existing society, in the industry based on individual exchanges, the anarchy of production, which is the source of so much misery, is at the same time the source of all progress.

Marx, 'Poverty of Philosophy' (1847)

In order to supersede the *idea* of private property, the *idea* of communism is enough. In order to supersede private property as it actually exists, *real* communist activity is necessary.

Marx, 'Economic and Philosophic Manuscripts' (1844; first published 1932)

Relations of personal dependence are the first social forms in which human productive capacity develops only to a slight extent and at isolated points. Personal independence founded on objective dependence is the second major form, in which a system of universal social metabolism, of general relations, of all-round needs and general capacities is formed for the first time. Free individuality, based on the universal development of individuals and on their subordination of their communal, social productivity as their social wealth, is the third stage.

Marx, 'Grundrisse' (1857; first published 1939)

If one class is to be the class of liberation *par excellence*, then another class must be the class of overt oppression.

Marx, 'Critique of Hegel's Philosophy of Right. Introduction.' (1844)

...private property ... is the very antithesis of a *social* relationship.

Marx, 'Excerpts from James Mill's *Elements of Political Economy*' (1844; first published 1932)

The modern bourgeois society that has sprouted from the ruins of feudal society has not done away with class antagonisms. It has but established new classes, new conditions of oppression, new forms of struggle in place of the old ones.

Marx & Engels, 'Communist Manifesto' (1848)

But generally speaking, the free trade system is destructive. It breaks up old nationalities and pushes the antagonism between proletariat and bourgeoisie to the uttermost point. In a word, the system of commercial freedom hastens the social revolution. It is in this revolutionary sense alone, gentlemen, I am in favour of free trade.

Marx, 'Speech on Free Trade' (1848)

A house may be large or small; as long as the neighbouring houses are likewise small, it satisfies all social requirement for a residence. But let there arise next to the little house a palace, and the little house shrinks to a hut. The little house now makes it clear that its inmate has no social position at all to maintain, or but a very insignificant one; and however high it may shoot up in the course of civilisation, if the neighbouring palace rises in equal or even in greater measure, the occupant of the relatively little house will always find himself more uncomfortable, more dissatisfied, more cramped within his four walls.

Marx, 'Wage Labour and Capital' (1847; first published 1849)

Morality, religion, metaphysics, and the rest of ideology and their corresponding forms of consciousness reserve here no longer the semblance of independence. They have no history, they have no development, but men, developing their material production and their material intercourse, change, with this their real existence, their thinking and the products of their thinking.

Marx & Engels, 'German Ideology' (1845-6; first published 1932)

We pre-suppose labour in a form that stamps it as exclusively human. A spider conducts operations that resemble those of a weaver, and a bee puts to shame many an architect in the construction of her cells. But what distinguishes the worst architect from the best of bees is this, that the architect raises his structure in imagination before he erects it in reality. At the end of every labour-process, we get a result that already existed in the imagination of the labourer at its commencement. He not only effects a change of form in the material on which he works, but he also realises a purpose of his own...

Marx, 'Capital, Volume I' (1867)

Between capitalist and communist society there lies the period of the revolutionary transformation of the one into the other. Corresponding to this is also a political transition period in which the state can be nothing but *the revolutionary dictatorship of the proletariat.*

Marx, 'Critique of the Gotha Programme' (1875; first published 1891)

Capital is dead labour, that, vampire-like, only lives by sucking living labour, and lives the more, the more labour it sucks. The time during which the labourer works, is the time during which the capitalist consumes the labour-power he has purchased of him.

Marx, 'Capital, Volume I' (1867)

A revolution is certainly the most authoritarian thing there is; it is the act whereby one part of the population imposes its will upon the other part by means of rifles, bayonets and cannon — authoritarian means, if such there be at all; and if the victorious party does not want to have fought in vain, it must maintain this rule by means of the terror which its arms inspire in the reactionists. Would the Paris Commune have lasted a single day if it had not made use of this authority of the armed people against the bourgeois? Should we not, on the contrary, reproach it for not having used it freely enough?

Engel, 'On Authority' (1872; first published 1874)

We know only a single science, the science of history. The story can be viewed from two sides, and divided into the history of nature and human history. Both sides are, however, inseparable; as long as people exist, the history of nature and history of the men are mutually dependent. The history of nature, the so-called science, we are not concerned with here; however we will have to examine the history of the men, since nearly the whole of ideology is reduced either to a twisted view of history or an utter abstraction from it. Ideology itself is only one of the aspects of this story.

Marx & Engels, 'German Ideology' (1845-6; first published 1932)

...consciousness takes the place of instinct...

Marx & Engels, 'German Ideology' (1845-6; first published 1932)

Productive labour is only that which produces *capital*.

Marx, 'Grundrisse' (1857; first published 1939)

All social life is essentially *practical*. All mysteries which lead theory to mysticism find their rational solution in human practice and in the comprehension of this practice.

Marx, 'Theses on Feuerbach: Thesis VIII' (1845; first published 1888)

...reciprocal dependence is expressed in the constant necessity for exchange, and in exchange value as the all-sided mediation. The economists express this as follows: Each pursues his private interest and solely his private interest; and thereby serves the private interests of all, the general interest, without willing or knowing it ... One could just as well deduce from this abstract phrase that each individual reciprocally blocks the assertion of the others' interests, so that, instead of a universal affirmation, this war of all against all produces a general negation. The point is rather that private interest is itself already a socially determined interest, which can be achieved only within the conditions laid down by society and with the means provided by society; thus it is bound to the reproduction of these conditions and means. It is the interest of private persons; but its content, as well as the form and means of its realisation, is given by social conditions independent of all.

Marx, 'Grundrisse' (1857; first published 1939)

The criminal produces an impression, partly moral and partly tragic, as the case may be, and in this way renders a "service" by arousing the moral and aesthetic feelings of the public. He produces not only compendia on Criminal Law, not only penal codes and along with them legislators in this field, but also art, *belles-lettres*, novels, and even tragedies ... The criminal breaks the monotony and everyday security of bourgeois life. In this way he keeps it from stagnation, and gives rise to that uneasy tension and agility without which even the spur of competition would get blunted. Thus he gives a stimulus to the productive forces. While crime takes a part of the superfluous population off the labour market and thus reduces competition among the labourers — up to a certain point preventing wages from falling below the minimum — the struggle against crime absorbs another part of this population. So the criminal comes in as one of those natural "counterweights" which bring about a correct balance and open up a whole perspective of "useful" occupations.

Marx, 'Theories of Surplus Value, Book One' (1861; first published 1905-10)

Man's reflections on the forms of social life, and consequently, also, his scientific analysis of those forms, take a course directly *opposite* to that of their actual historical development. He begins, *post festum*, with the results of the process of development ready to hand before him.

Marx, 'Capital, Volume I' (1867)

...the existence of the things *qua* commodities, and the value-relation between the products of labour which stamps them as commodities, have absolutely no connection with their physical properties and with the material relations arising therefrom. There it is a definite social relation between men, which assumes, in their eyes, the fantastic form of a *relation between things* ... This I call the *fetishism* ... of commodities.

Marx, 'Capital, Volume I' (1867)

Violations of the law are generally the offspring of economical agencies ... it depends to some degree on official society to stamp certain violations of its rules as crimes or as transgressions only. This difference of nomenclature, so far from being indifferent, decides on the fate of thousands of men, and the moral tone of society. Law itself may not only punish crime, but improvise it...

Marx, 'Population, Crime, and Pauperism' article in the *New-York Daily Tribune*, (1859)

Each new class, namely the one which sits itself in the place of one ruling before it, is compelled, in order to carry out its purpose, to represent their interest as the common interest of all members of society, i.e., expressed ideologically: to give their ideas the form of universality, to represent them as the only rational, universally valid ones.

Marx & Engels, 'German Ideology' (1845-6; first published 1932)

Production creates the objects which correspond to the given needs; distribution divides them up according to social laws; exchange further parcels out the already divided shares in accord with individual needs; and finally, in consumption, the product steps outside this social movement and becomes a direct object and servant of individual need, and satisfies it in being consumed. Hence production appears as the starting-point, consumption as the conclusion, distribution and exchange as the middle, which is however itself twofold, since distribution is determined by society and exchange by individuals.

Marx, 'Grundrisse' (1857; first published 1939)

It is with man as with commodities. Since he comes into the world neither with a looking glass in his hand, nor as a Fichtean philosopher, to whom 'I am I' is sufficient, man first sees and recognises himself in other men. Peter only establishes his own identity as a man by first comparing himself with Paul as being of like kind. And thereby Paul, just as he stands in his Pauline personality, becomes to Peter the type of the genus *homo*.

Marx, 'Capital, Volume I' (1867)

Political economy proceeds from the fact of private property. It does not explain it.

Marx, 'Economic and Philosophic Manuscripts' (1844; first published 1932)

Political Economy has indeed analysed, however incompletely, value and its magnitude, and has discovered what lies beneath these forms. But it has never once asked the question why labour is represented by the value of its product and labour-time by the magnitude of that value. These formulae, which bear it stamped upon them in unmistakable letters that they belong to a state of society, in which the process of production has the mastery over man, instead of being controlled by him, such formulae appear to the bourgeois intellect to be as much a self-evident necessity imposed by Nature as productive labour itself.

Marx, 'Capital, Volume I' (1867)

A man cannot become a child again, or he becomes childish. But does he not find joy in the child's naïveté, and must he himself not strive to reproduce its truth at a higher stage? Does not the true character of each epoch come alive in the nature of its children? Why should not the historic childhood of humanity, its most beautiful unfolding, as a stage never to return, exercise a timeless allure?

Marx, 'Grundrisse' (1857; first published 1939)

Love first really teaches a man to believe in the objective world outside himself. It not only makes man the object but the object a man. Love makes the beloved into an external object, a sensuous object which does not remain internal, hidden in the brain.

Marx & Engels, 'The Holy Family' (1845)

The price or money-form of commodities is, like their form of value generally, a form quite distinct from their palpable bodily form; it is, therefore, a purely ideal or mental form.

Marx, 'Capital, Volume I' (1867)

Division of labour and private property are, furthermore, identical expressions: in the one the same thing is affirmed with reference to activity as is affirmed in the other with reference to the product of the activity.

Marx & Engels, 'German Ideology' (1845-6; first published 1932)

An oppressed class is the vital condition of every society based upon the antagonism of classes. The emancipation of the oppressed class therefore necessarily implies the creation of a new society. In order for the new oppressed class to be emancipated it is necessary that the productive powers already acquired and the existing social relations should no longer be able to exist side by side. Of all the instruments of production the greatest productive power is the revolutionary class itself.

Marx, 'Poverty of Philosophy' (1847)

Modern society, which, soon after its birth, pulled Plutus by the hair of his head from the bowels of the earth, greets gold as its Holy Grail, as the glittering incarnation of the very principle of its own life.

Marx, 'Capital, Volume I' (1867)

History does *nothing*, it 'possesses *no* immense wealth', it 'wages *no* battles'. It is *man*, real, living man who does all that, who possesses and fights; 'history' is not, as it were, a person apart, using man as a means to achieve *its own* aims; history is *nothing but* the activity of man pursuing his aims.

Marx & Engels, 'The Holy Family' (1845)

The *free labourer* ... sells at auction eight, ten, twelve, fifteen hours of his life, day after day, to the highest bidder, to ... the capitalist. The worker belongs neither to an owner nor to the land, but eight, ten, twelve, fifteen hours of his daily life belong to him who buys them. The worker leaves the capitalist to whom he hires himself whenever he likes, and the capitalist discharges him whenever he thinks fit, as soon as he no longer gets any profit out of him, or not the anticipated profit.

Marx, 'Wage Labour and Capital' (1847; first published 1849)

To sum up, what is free trade under the present conditions of society? It is freedom of capital. When you have torn down the few national barriers which still restrict the free development of capital, you will merely have given it complete freedom of action. So long as the relation of wage-labour to capital is permitted to exist, no matter how favourable the conditions under which you accomplish the exchange of commodities, there will always be a class which exploits and a class which is exploited.

Marx, 'Speech on Free Trade' (1848)

It seems to be correct to begin with the actual and the concrete, with the real precondition, thus to begin, in economics, with e.g. the population, which is the foundation and the subject of the entire social act of production. However, on closer examination this proves wrong. The population is an *abstraction* if I leave out, for example, the classes of which it is composed ... if I were to begin with the population, this would be a chaotic conception of the whole, and I would then, by means of further determination, move analytically towards ever more simple concepts, from the imagined concrete towards ever thinner abstractions until I had arrived at the simplest determinations. From there the journey would have to be retraced until I had finally arrived at the population again, but this time not as the chaotic conception of a whole, but as a rich totality of many determinations and relations.

Marx, 'Grundrisse' (1857; first published 1939)

But the worker, whose sole source of livelihood is the sale of his labour, cannot leave the *whole class of purchasers, that is, the capitalist class*, without renouncing his existence. *He belongs not to this or that bourgeois, but to the bourgeoisie, the bourgeois class*, and it is his business to dispose to himself, that is to find a purchaser within this bourgeois class.

Marx, 'Wage Labour and Capital' (1847; first published 1849)

Bourgeois society is the most advanced and the most complex historic organisation of production.

Marx, 'Grundrisse' (1857; first published 1939)

In every stock-jobbing swindle everyone knows that some time or other the crash must come, but every one hopes that it may fall on the head of his neighbour, after he himself has caught the shower of gold and placed it in safety. *Après moi le déluge*! is the watchword of every capitalist and of every capitalist nation. Hence Capital is reckless of the health or length of life of the labourer, unless under compulsion from society.

Marx, 'Capital, Volume I' (1867)

...the State has become a separate entity, beside and outside civil society; but it is nothing more than the form of organisation which the bourgeois necessarily give themselves both for foreign and domestic purposes, for the mutual guarantee of their property and interests.

Marx & Engels, 'German Ideology' (1845-6; first published 1932)

That which comes directly face to face with the possessor of money on the market, is in fact not labour, but the labourer. What the latter sells is his *labour-power*. As soon as his labour actually begins, it has already ceased to belong to him; it can therefore no longer be sold by him. Labour is the substance, and the immanent measure of value, but has itself no value ... That in their appearance things often represent themselves in inverted form is pretty well known in every science except Political Economy.

Marx, 'Capital, Volume I' (1867)

...in communist society, where nobody has one exclusive sphere of activity but can develop in any branch, society administers production generally and thus makes it possible for me to do one thing today and another tomorrow, to hunt in the morning, fish in the afternoon, rear cattle in the evening, criticise after dinner, as I have a mind to be, without ever becoming hunter, fisherman, shepherd or critic.

Marx & Engels, 'German Ideology' (1845-6; first published 1932)

So long as the proletariat is not sufficiently developed to constitute itself as a class ... in consequence, the struggle between the proletariat and the bourgeoisie has not acquired a political character ...

Marx, 'Poverty of Philosophy' (1847)

The bourgeoisie, historically, has played a most revolutionary part.

Marx & Engels, 'Communist Manifesto' (1848)

Capitalist production is not merely the production of commodities, it is essentially the production of surplus-value. The labourer produces, not for himself, but for capital ... That labourer alone is productive, who produces surplus-value for the capitalist, and thus works for the self-expansion of capital.

Marx, 'Capital, Volume I' (1867)

Fanatically bent on making value expand itself, he ruthlessly forces the human race to produce for production's sake; he thus forces the development of the productive powers of society, and creates those material conditions, which alone can form the real basis of a higher form of society, a society in which the full and free development of every individual forms the ruling principle.

Marx, 'Capital, Volume I' (1867)

Political Economy can remain a science only so long as the class-struggle is latent or manifests itself only in isolated and sporadic phenomena ... In France and in England the bourgeoisie had conquered political power. Thenceforth, the class-struggle, practically as well as theoretically, took on more and more outspoken and threatening forms. It sounded the knell of scientific bourgeois economy. It was thenceforth no longer a question, whether this theorem or that was true, but whether it was useful to capital or harmful, expedient or inexpedient, politically dangerous or not. In place of disinterested inquirers, there were hired prize fighters; in place of genuine scientific research, the bad conscience and the evil intent of apologetic.

Marx, 'Afterword' to the second German edition of *Capital, Vol. I* (1873)

...capitalist production begets, with the inexorability of a law of Nature, its own negation. It is the negation of negation.

Marx, 'Capital, Volume I' (1867)

A commodity appears, at first sight, a very trivial thing, and easily understood. Its analysis shows that it is, in reality, a very queer thing, abounding in metaphysical subtleties and theological niceties.

Marx, 'Capital, Volume I' (1867)

The relations of production of every society form a whole.

Marx, 'Poverty of Philosophy' (1847)

For philosophers, one of the most difficult tasks is to descend from the world of ideas to the real world. *Language* is the immediate actuality of thought. Just as philosophers have given thought an independent existence, so they were bound to make language into an independent realm.

Marx & Engels, 'German Ideology' (1845-6; first published 1932)

The secret of the expression of value, namely, that all kinds of labour are equal and equivalent, because, and so far as they are human labour in general, cannot be deciphered, until the notion of human equality has already acquired the fixity of a popular prejudice. This, however, is possible only in a society in which the great mass of the produce of labour takes the form of commodities, in which, consequently, the dominant relation between man and man, is that of owners of commodities.

Marx, 'Capital, Volume I' (1867)

A. Smith was *essentially* correct with his *productive* and *unproductive* labour, correct from the standpoint of bourgeois economy. What the other economists advance against it is either horse-piss ... Or the modern economists have turned themselves into such sycophants of the bourgeois ... The fact is that these workers, indeed, are productive, as far as they increase the capital of their master; unproductive as to the material result of their labour. In fact, of course, this 'productive' worker cares as little about the crappy shit he has to make as does the capitalist himself who employs him, and who couldn't give a damn for the rubbish. But, looked at more precisely, it turns out in fact that the true definition of a productive worker consists in this: A person who needs and demands exactly as much as, and no more than, is required to enable him to gain the greatest possible benefit for his capitalist.

Marx, 'Grundrisse' (1857; first published 1939)

While the miser is merely a capitalist gone mad, the capitalist is a rational miser.

Marx, 'Capital, Volume I' (1867)

A really human morality which stands above class antagonisms and above any recollection of them becomes possible only at a stage of society which has not only overcome class antagonisms but has even forgotten them in practical life.

Engels, 'Anti-Dühring' (1877)

In short, by the introduction of machinery the division of labour within society has been developed, the task of the workman ... has been simplified, capital has been accumulated, and man has been further dismembered.

Marx, 'Poverty of Philosophy' (1847)

...a schoolmaster is a productive labourer when, in addition to belabouring the heads of his scholars, he works like a horse to enrich the school proprietor. That the latter has laid out his capital in a teaching factory, instead of in a sausage factory, does not alter the relation.

Marx, 'Capital, Volume I' (1867)

Anyone who has any knowledge of the statistics of crime must be struck by the peculiar regularity with which certain causes produce certain crimes ... This regularity proves that crime, too, is governed by competition, that society creates a *demand* for crime which is met by a corresponding supply.

Engels, 'Outlines of a Critique Political Economy' (1844)

Capitalist production, therefore, develops technology, and the combining together of various processes into a social whole, only by sapping the original sources of all wealth – the soil and the labourer.

Marx, 'Capital, Volume I' (1867)

The social relations are intimately attached to the productive forces. In acquiring new productive forces men change their mode of production, and in changing their mode of production, their manner of gaining a living, they change all their social relations.

Marx, 'Poverty of Philosophy' (1847)

The slave frees himself when, of all the relations of private property, he abolishes only the relation of slavery and thereby becomes a proletarian; the proletarian can free himself only by *abolishing private property in general*.

Engels, 'Principles of Communism' (1847; first published 1914)

Our desires and pleasures spring from society; we measure them, therefore, by society and not by the objects which serve for their satisfaction. Because they are of a social nature, they are of a relative nature.

Marx, 'Wage Labour and Capital' (1847; first published 1849)

...the principles are not the starting-point of the investigation, but its final result; they are not applied to nature and human history, but abstracted from them, it is not nature and the realm of man which conform to these principles, but the principles are only valid in so far as they are in conformity with nature and history. That is the only materialist conception of the matter.

Engels, 'Anti-Dühring' (1877)

For ... the proletarians, to affirm themselves as individuals, will at the same time have to repeal the previous condition of their existence, and of all hitherto existing society, namely, labour. They therefore are in direct opposition to the form in which the individuals, of which society consists, so far gave a collective expression, that is, the State, and to empower themselves as individuals they must overthrow the State.

Marx & Engels, 'German Ideology' (1845-6; first published 1932)

My dialectic method is not only different from the Hegelian, but is its direct opposite ... With him it is standing on its head. It must be turned right side up again, if you would discover the rational kernel within the mystical shell.

Marx, 'Afterword' to the second German edition of *Capital, Vol. I* (1873)

The categories of bourgeois economy consist of such like forms. They are forms of thought expressing with social validity the conditions and relations of a definite, historically determined mode of production, viz., the production of commodities. The whole mystery of commodities, all the magic and necromancy that surrounds the products of labour as long as they take the form of commodities, vanishes therefore, so soon as we come to other forms of production.

Marx, 'Capital, Volume I' (1867)

Labour is ... not the only source of material wealth, i.e. of the use-values it produces. As William Petty says, labour is the father of material wealth, the earth is its mother.

Marx, 'Capital, Volume I' (1867)

The domination of capital has created for this mass of people a common situation with common interests. Thus this mass is already a class, as opposed to capital, but not yet for itself. In the struggle, of which we have noted some phases, this mass unites, it is constituted as a class for itself. The interests which it defends are the interests of its class.

Marx, 'Poverty of Philosophy' (1847)

...a class is called forth, which has to bear all the burdens of society without enjoying its advantages, which, expelled from society, is forced into the most decided antagonism to all other classes; a class which forms the majority of all members of society, and from the awareness of the need for a thorough revolution, the communist consciousness emanates...

Marx & Engels, 'German Ideology' (1845-6; first published 1932)

...two contradictory thoughts, the positive and the negative, the yes and no. The struggle of these two antagonistic elements, comprised in the antithesis, constitutes the dialectic movement.

Marx, 'Poverty of Philosophy' (1847)

The exclusive concentration of artistic talent in particular individuals, and its suppression in the broad mass which is bound up with this, is a consequence of division of labour ... In a communist society there are no painters but at most people who engage in paining among other activities.

Marx & Engels, 'German Ideology' (1845-6; first published 1932)

What the bourgeoisie, therefore, produces, above all, is its own grave-diggers. Its fall and the victory of the proletariat are equally inevitable.

Marx & Engels, 'Communist Manifesto' (1848)

There are characteristics which all stages of production have in common, and which are established as universal ones by the mind; but the so-called *universal preconditions* of all production are nothing more than these abstract moments with which no actual historical stage of production can be grasped.

Marx, 'Grundrisse' (1857; first published 1939)

As capitalist, he is only capital personified. His soul is the soul of capital. But capital has one single life impulse, the tendency to create value and surplus-value, to make its constant factor, the means of production, absorb the greatest possible amount of surplus-labour.

Marx, 'Capital, Volume I' (1867)

Capital is money: Capital is commodities ... Because it is value, it has acquired the occult quality of being able to add value to itself. It brings forth living offspring, or, at the least, lays golden eggs.

Marx, 'Capital, Volume I' (1867)

The *human* essence of nature exists only for *social* man because only here does it exist for him as a *bond* with other *people*, as his existence for others and their existence for him, as a vital element of human reality; only here does it exist as the *basis* of his own *human* existence. Only here has his *natural* existence become his *human* existence and nature become human for him. *Society* is therefore the consummate unity in essence of man with nature, the true resurrection of nature, the realised naturalism of man and the realised humanism of nature.

Marx, 'Economic and Philosophic Manuscripts' (1844; first published 1932)

...the communist revolution is directed against the preceding *mode* of activity, does away with [the division of] labour, and abolishes the rule of all classes with the classes themselves, because it is carried through by the class not recognised as a class, yet which is the most important in society as it is the expression of the dissolution of all classes, nationalities, etc. within present society.

Marx & Engels, 'German Ideology' (1845-6; first published 1932)

Men make their own history, but they do not make it as they please; not under circumstances they themselves have chosen but under the given and inherited circumstances transmitted from the past. The tradition of all dead generations weighs like a nightmare on the minds of the living.

Marx, 'The Eighteenth Brumaire of Louis Bonaparte' (1852)

In the course of its historical development, the bourgeoisie necessarily develops its antagonistic character, which at its first appearance was found to be more or less disguised, and existed only in a latent state. In proportion as the bourgeoisie develops, it develops in its bosom a new proletariat, a modern proletariat: it develops a struggle between the proletarian class and the bourgeois class, a struggle which, before it is felt, perceived, appreciated, comprehended, avowed and loudly proclaimed by the two sides, only manifests itself previously by partial and momentary conflicts, by subversive acts.

Marx, 'Poverty of Philosophy' (1847)

Capital can only increase by exchanging itself for labour, by calling wage labour to life. The wage labour can only be exchanged for capital by increasing capital, by strengthening the power whose slave it is. *Hence, increase of capital is increase of the proletariat, that is, of the working class.*

Marx, 'Wage Labour and Capital' (1847; first published 1849)

Man makes his life activity itself the object of his will and consciousness. He has conscious life activity. It is not a determination with which he merges immediately. Conscious life activity instantly distinguishes man from animal life activity. Only because of that is he a species-being. Or rather, he is a conscious being, i.e. his own life is an object for him, precisely because he is a species-being. Only because of that is his activity free activity. Estranged labour reverses the relationship so that man, just because he is a conscious being, makes his life activity, his *essence*, a mere means for his *existence*.

Marx, 'Economic and Philosophic Manuscripts' (1844; first published 1932)

The Communists are further reproached with desiring to abolish countries and nationality … The working men have no country. We cannot take from them what they have not got. Since the proletariat must first of all acquire political supremacy, must rise to be the leading class of the nation, must constitute itself *the* nation, it is, so far, itself national, though not in the bourgeois sense of the word.

Marx & Engels, 'Communist Manifesto' (1848)

The different proportions in which different sorts of labour are reduced to unskilled labour as their standard, are established by a social process that goes on behind the backs of the producers, and, consequently, appear to be fixed by custom.

Marx, 'Capital, Volume I' (1867)

By selling, therefore, the commodity *at its value*, that is, as the crystallisation of the *total quantity of labour* bestowed upon it, the capitalist must necessarily sell it at a profit ... I repeat, therefore, that normal and average profits are made by selling commodities not *above* but *at their real values*.

Marx, 'Value, Price and Profit' (1865; first published 1898)

The history of all hitherto existing society is the history of class struggles.

Marx & Engels, 'Communist Manifesto' (1848)

Although jurisprudence was my special study, I pursued it as a subject subordinated to philosophy and history. In the year 1842-43, as editor of *Rheinische Zeitung*, I first found myself in the embarrassing position of having to discuss what is known as material interests ... [this] caused me in the first instance to turn my attention to economic questions.

Marx, 'Preface' to *A Contribution to the Critique of Political Economy* (1859)

The bourgeoisie has stripped of its halo every occupation hitherto honoured and looked up to with reverent awe. It has converted the physician, the lawyer, the priest, the poet, the man of science, into its paid wage-labourers.

Marx & Engels, 'Communist Manifesto' (1848)

Philosophy and the study of the actual world have the same relation to one another as masturbation and sexual love.

Marx & Engels, 'German Ideology' (1845-6; first published 1932)

What is Communism? Communism is the doctrine of the conditions of the liberation of the proletariat. What is the proletariat? The proletariat is that class in society which lives entirely from the sale of its labour and does not draw profit from any kind of capital; whose weal and woe, whose life and death, whose sole existence depends on the demand for labour...

Engels, 'Principles of Communism' (1847; first published 1914)

Individuals … stand not only in an equivalent, but also in a social, relation to one another. This is not all. The fact that the need on the part of one can be satisfied by the product of the other, and vice versa, and that the one is capable of producing the object of the need of the other, and that each confronts the other as owner of the object of the other's need, this proves that each of them reaches beyond his own particular need, etc., as an *individual being*, and that they relate to one another as human beings; that their common species-being is acknowledged by all. It does not happen elsewhere – that elephants produce for tigers, or animals for other animals.

Marx, 'Grundrisse' (1857; first published 1939)

To explain ... the *general nature of profits*, you must start from the theorem that, on an average, commodities are *sold at their real value*, and that *profits are derived from selling them at their values*, that is, in proportion to the quantity of labour realised in them. If you cannot explain profit upon this supposition, you cannot explain it at all. This seems paradox and contrary to everyday observation. It is also paradox that the earth moves round the sun, and that water consists of two highly inflammable gases. Scientific truth is always paradox, if judged by everyday experience, which catches only the delusive appearance of things.

Marx, 'Value, Price and Profit' (1865; first published 1898)

...it is only possible to achieve real liberation in the real world by employing real means ... in general, men cannot be liberated as long as they are unable to obtain food and drink, housing and clothing in adequate quality and quantity. "Liberation" is an historical and not a mental act...

Marx & Engels, 'German Ideology' (1845-6; first published 1932)

It establishes an accumulation of misery, corresponding with accumulation of capital. Accumulation of wealth at one pole is, therefore, at the same time accumulation of misery, agony of toil slavery, ignorance, brutality, mental degradation, at the opposite pole, i.e. on the side of the class the produces its own product in the form of capital.

Marx, 'Capital, Volume I' (1867)

A man who has no free time to dispose of, whose whole lifetime, apart from the mere physical interruptions by sleep, meals, and so forth, is absorbed by his labour for the capitalist, is less than a beast of burden. He is a mere machine for producing Foreign Wealth, broken in body and brutalised in mind. Yet the whole history of modern industry shows that capital, if not checked, will recklessly and ruthlessly work to cast down the whole working class to the utmost state of degradation.

Marx, 'Value, Price and Profit' (1865; first published 1898)

Under the freedom of trade the whole severity of the laws of political economy will be applied to the working classes. Is that to say that we are against Free Trade? No, we are for Free Trade, because by Free Trade all economical laws, with their most astounding contradictions, will act upon a larger scale, upon a greater extent of territory, upon the territory of the whole earth; and because from the uniting of all these contradictions into a single group, where they stand face to face, will result the struggle which will itself eventuate in the emancipation of the proletarians.

Engels, 'Free Trade Congress at Brussels' (1847; first published 1848)

Newton's discovery of the binomial (in his application, also the polynomial) theorem revolutionised the whole of algebra, since it made possible for the first time a *general theory of equations*.

Marx, 'Mathematical Manuscripts' (1881; first published 1933)

Of course the method of presentation must differ in form from that of inquiry. The latter has to appropriate the material in detail, to analyse its different forms of development, to trace out their inner connexion. Only after this work is done, can the actual movement be adequately described. If this is done successfully, if the life of the subject-matter is ideally reflected as in a mirror, then it may appear as if we had before us a mere *a priori* construction.

Marx, 'Afterword' to the second German edition of *Capital, Vol. I* (1873)

In reality and for the *practical* materialist, i.e. the *communist*, it is a question of revolutionising the existing world, of practically attacking the encountered and changing things.

Marx & Engels, 'German Ideology' (1845-6; first published 1932)

Punishment in general has been defended as a means either of ameliorating or of intimidating. Now what right have you to punish me for the amelioration or intimidation of others? And besides, there is history — there is such a thing as statistics — which prove with the most complete evidence that since Cain the world has neither been intimidated nor ameliorated by punishment … Plainly speaking, and dispensing with all paraphrases, punishment is nothing but a means of society to defend itself against the infraction of its vital conditions, whatever may be their character.

Marx, 'Capital Punishment' article in the *New-York Daily Tribune* (1853)

The conclusion we reach is not that production, distribution, exchange and consumption are identical, but that they all form the parts of a totality, distinctions within a unity. Production predominates not only over itself, in the antithetical definition of production, but over the other moments as well. The process always returns to production to begin anew.

Marx, 'Grundrisse' (1857; first published 1939)

Every step of real movement is more important than a dozen programmes.

Marx, 'Letter to Bracke' (1875; first published 1890-91)

Within communist society, the only society in which the original and free development of men ceases to be a mere phrase, this development is determined precisely by the connection of men, a connection which consists partly in the economic prerequisites and partly in the necessary solidarity of the free development of all, and, finally, in the universal character of the activity of men on the basis of the existing forces of production.

Marx & Engels, 'German Ideology' (1845-6; first published 1932)

To leave error unrefuted is to encourage intellectual immorality.

Marx, in conversation with Hyndman (1881; first published 1911)

One has to "leave philosophy aside", one has to leap out of it and devote oneself like an ordinary man to the study of reality...

Marx & Engels, 'German Ideology' (1845-6; first published 1932)

Economists explain how production takes place in the above-mentioned relations, but what they do not explain is how these relations themselves are produced, that is, the historical movement which gave them birth.

Marx, 'Poverty of Philosophy' (1847)

The distinguishing feature of Communism is not the abolition of property generally, but the abolition of bourgeois property ... In this sense, the theory of the Communists may be summed up in a single sentence: Abolition of private property.

Marx & Engels, 'Communist Manifesto' (1848)

There must be something rotten in the very core of a social system which increases its wealth without diminishing its misery...

Marx, 'Population, Crime and Pauperism' article in *New-York Daily Tribune* (1859)

Human anatomy contains a key to the anatomy of the ape.

Marx, 'Grundrisse' (1857; first published 1939)

Like that of every other commodity, [the value of labouring power] is determined by the quantity of labour necessary to produce it … A certain mass of necessaries must be consumed by a man to grow up and maintain his life … Moreover, to develop his labouring power, and acquire a given skill, another amount of values must be spent … the *value of labouring power* is determined by the *value of the necessaries* required to produce, develop, maintain, and perpetuate the labouring power.

Marx, 'Value, Price and Profit' (1865; first published 1898)

But the working class cannot simply lay hold of the ready-made state machinery, and wield it for its own purposes.

Marx, 'The Civil War in France' (1871)

Nature is the proof of dialectics, and it must be said for modern science that it has furnished this proof with very rich materials increasingly daily, and thus has shown that, in the last resort, Nature works dialectically and not metaphysically; that she does not move in the eternal oneness of a perpetually recurring circle, but goes through a real historical evolution.

Engels, 'Socialism: Utopian & Scientific' (1880)

Instead of deciding once in three or six years which member of the ruling class was to misrepresent the people in parliament, universal suffrage was to serve the people...

Marx, 'The Civil War in France' (1871)

The workers will have to seize political power one day in order to construct the new organisation of labour; they will have to overthrow the old politics which bolster up the old institutions ... We do not claim, however, that the road leading to this goal is the same everywhere.

We know that heed must be paid to the institutions, customs and traditions of the various countries, and we do not deny that there are countries, such as America and England ... where the workers may attain their goals by peaceful means. But this is not the case in all countries.

Marx, 'Speech on the Hague Congress' (1872)

...communism is only possible as the act of the dominant peoples "all at once" and simultaneously, which presupposes the universal development of productive forces and the world intercourse bound up with communism.

Marx & Engels, 'German Ideology' (1845-6; first published 1932)

What is a Negro slave? A man of the black race ... A Negro is a Negro. He only becomes a *slave* in certain relations. A cotton-spinning machine is a machine for spinning cotton. It becomes capital only in certain relations. Torn away from these relations, it is no more capital than *gold* in itself is *money*, or sugar is the price of sugar.

Marx, 'Wage Labour and Capital' (1847; first published 1849)

The directing motive, the end and aim of capitalist production, is to extract the greatest possible amount of surplus-value, and consequently to exploit labour-power to the greatest possible extent.

Marx, 'Capital, Volume I' (1867)

The worst thing that can befall a leader of an extreme party is to be compelled to take over a government in an epoch when the movement is not yet ripe for the domination of the class which he represents and for the realisation of the measures which that domination would imply...

Engels, 'The Peasant War in Germany' (1850)

Surplus value in general is value in excess of the equivalent. The equivalent, by definition, is only the identity of value with itself. Hence surplus value can never sprout out of the equivalent; nor can it do so originally out of circulation; it has to arise from the production process of capital itself.

Marx, 'Grundrisse' (1857; first published 1939)

A rise in the price of labour, as a consequence of accumulation of capital, only means, in fact, that the length and weight of the golden chain the wage-worker has already forged for himself, allow of a relaxation of the tension of it.

Marx, 'Capital, Volume I' (1867)

In a real community the individuals obtain their freedom in and through their association.

Marx & Engels, 'German Ideology' (1845-6; first published 1932)

...in a society based upon *poverty*, the *poorest* products have the fatal prerogative of serving the use of the greatest number.

Marx, 'Poverty of Philosophy' (1847)

Labour is ... the worker's own life-activity, the manifestation of his own life. And this *life-activity* he sells to another person in order to secure the necessary *means of subsistence*. Thus his life-activity is for him only a *means* to enable him to exist. He works in order to live. He does not even reckon labour as part of his life, it is rather a sacrifice of his life.

Marx, 'Wage Labour and Capital' (1847; first published 1849)

It is enough to mention the commercial crisis that by their periodical return put on its trial, each time more threateningly, the existence of the entire bourgeois society. In these crisis a great part of not only of the existing products, but also of the previously created productive forces, are periodically destroyed. In these crisis there breaks out an epidemic that, in all earlier epochs, would have seemed an absurdity – the epidemic of over-production.

Marx & Engels, 'Communist Manifesto' (1848)

...how ridiculous is the conception of history held previously, which neglects the real relationships and confines itself to high-sounding dramas of princes and states.

Marx & Engels, 'German Ideology' (1845-6; first published 1932)

...the highest development of productive power together with the greatest expansion of existing wealth will coincide with depreciation of capital, degradation of the labourer, and a most straitened exhaustion of his vital powers. These contradictions lead to explosions, cataclysms, crisis, in which by momentaneous suspension of labour and annihilation of a great portion of capital the latter is violently reduced to the point where it can go on ... Yet, these regularly recurring catastrophes lead to their repetition on a higher scale, and finally to its violent overthrow.

Marx, 'Grundrisse' (1857; first published 1939)

What we are dealing with here is a communist society, not as it has *developed* on its own foundations, but on the contrary, just as it *emerges* from capitalist society, which is thus in every respect, economically, morally, and intellectually, still stamped with the birth-marks of the old society from whose womb it emerges. Accordingly, the individual producer receives back from society – after deductions have been made – exactly what he gives to it.

Marx, 'Critique of the Gotha Programme' (1875; first published 1891)

In studying such transformations it is always necessary to distinguish between the material transformation of the economic conditions of production, which can be determined with the precision of natural science, and the legal, political, religious, artistic or philosophic – in short, ideological forms in which men become conscious of this conflict and fight it out.

Marx, 'Preface' to *A Contribution to the Critique of Political Economy* (1859)

…the abolition of this state of things is determined in the final analysis by the abolition of division of labour.

Marx & Engels, 'German Ideology' (1845-6; first published 1932)

The simple fact that every succeeding generation finds productive forces acquired by the preceding generation and which serve it as the raw material of further production, engenders a relatedness in the history of man, engenders a history of mankind, which is all the more a history of mankind as man's productive forces, and hence his social relations, have expanded. From this it can only be concluded that the social history of man is never anything else than the history of his individual development, whether he is conscious of this or not. His material relations form the basis of all his relations. These material relations are but the necessary forms in which his material and individual activity is realised.

Marx, 'Letter to Annenkov' (1846; first published 1912)

Is man free to choose this or that form of society? By no means. If you assume a given state of development of man's productive faculties, you will have a corresponding form of commerce or consumption. If you assume given stages of development in production, commerce or consumption, you will have a corresponding form of social constitution, a corresponding organisation, whether of the family, of the estates or of classes – in a word, a corresponding civil society. If you assume this or that civil society, you will have this or that political system, which is but the official expression of civil society.

Marx, 'Letter to Annenkov' (1846; first published 1912)

In production, men enter into relation not only with nature. They produce only by cooperating in a certain way and mutually exchanging their activities. In order to produce, they enter into definite connections and relations with one another and only within these social connections and relations does their relation with nature, does production, take place.

Marx, 'Wage Labour and Capital' (1847; first published 1849)

Capitalist production only then really begins ... when each individual capital employs simultaneously a comparatively large number of labourers; when consequently the labour-process is carried on on an extensive scale and yields, relatively, large quantities of products.

Marx, 'Capital, Volume I' (1867)

Although one part only of the workman's daily labour is *paid*, while the other part is *unpaid*, and while that unpaid or surplus-labour constitutes exactly the fund out of which *surplus-value* or *profit* is formed, it seems as if the aggregate labour was paid labour … The *surplus-value*, or that part of the total value of the commodity in which the *surplus-labour* or *unpaid labour* of the working man is realised, I call *Profit*.

Marx, 'Value, Price and Profit' (1865; first published 1898)

Society does not consist of individuals, but expresses the sum of interrelations, the relations within which these individuals stand. As if someone were to say: Seen from the viewpoint of society, there are no slaves and no citizens: both are men. Rather, they are that *outside* society. To be a slave, to be a citizen, are social determinations, relations between Man A and Man B. Man A is not a slave as such. He is a slave within and through society.

Marx, 'Grundrisse' (1857; first published 1939)

…here individuals are dealt with only in so far as they are the personifications of economic categories, embodiments of particular class-relations and class-interests. My standpoint, from which the evolution of the economic formation of society is viewed as a process of natural history, can less than any other make the individual responsible for relations whose creature he socially remains, however much he may subjectively raise himself above them.

Marx, 'Preface' to the first German edition of *Capital, Vol. I* (1867)

This expropriation is accomplished by the action of the immanent laws of capitalist production itself, by the centralisation of capital. One capitalist always kills many. Hand in hand with this centralisation, or this expropriation of many capitals by few, develop, on an ever-extending scale, the cooperative form of the labour-process ... the transformation of the instruments of labour into instruments of labour only usable in common, the economising of all means of production by their use as the means of production of combined, socialised labour, the entanglement of all peoples in the net of the world market, and with this, the international character of the capitalist regime.

Marx, 'Capital, Volume I' (1867)

The materialist doctrine concerning the changing of circumstances and upbringing forgets that circumstances are changed by men and that it is essential to educate the educator himself.

Marx, 'Theses on Feuerbach: Thesis III' (1845; first published 1888)

Along with the constantly diminishing number of the magnates of capital, who usurp and monopolise all advantages of this process of transformation, grows the mass of misery, oppression, slavery, degradation, exploitation; but with this too grows the revolt of the working class, a class always increasing in numbers, and disciplined, united, organised by the very mechanism of the process of capitalist production itself.

Marx, 'Capital, Volume I' (1867)

...crime [is] the struggle of the isolated individual against the prevailing conditions...

Marx & Engels, 'German Ideology' (1845-6; first published 1932)

Capital grows in one place to a huge mass in a single hand, because it has in another place been lost by many. This is centralisation proper, as distinct from accumulation and concentration.

Marx, 'Capital, Volume I' (1867)

Wages are only a special name for the *price of labour*, for the price of this peculiar commodity which has no other repository than human flesh and blood.

Marx, 'Wage Labour and Capital' (1847; first published 1849)

...all the members of the modern bourgeoisie have an identity of interest, inasmuch as they form a class opposed by another class, they have also conflicting, antagonistic interests, inasmuch as they find themselves opposed by each other. This opposition of interests flows from the economic conditions of their bourgeois life.

Marx, 'Poverty of Philosophy' (1847)

The existence of a class which possesses nothing but its capacity to labour is a necessary prerequisite of capital.

Marx, 'Wage Labour and Capital' (1847; first published 1849)

Whenever we speak of production, then, what is always meant is production at a definite stage of social development – production by social individuals. It might seem, therefore, that in order to talk about production at all we must either pursue the process of historic development through its different phases, or declare beforehand that we are dealing with a specific historic epoch such as e.g. modern bourgeois production, which is indeed our particular theme.

Marx, 'Grundrisse' (1857; first published 1939)

…it would be very difficult, if not altogether impossible, to establish any principle upon which the justice or expediency of capital punishment could be founded, in a society glorying in its civilization.

Marx, 'Capital Punishment' article in the *New-York Daily Tribune* (1853)

It is, therefore, from the history of nature and human society that the laws of dialectics are abstracted. For they are nothing but the most general laws of these two aspects of historical development, as well as of thought itself.

And indeed they can be reduced in the main to three: The law of the transformation of quantity into quality and vice versa; the law of the interpenetration of opposites; the law of the negation of the negation.

Engels, 'Dialectics of Nature' (1883; first published 1925)

Such are the various working-people's quarters of Manchester as I had occasion to observe them personally during twenty months. If we briefly formulate the result of our wanderings, we must admit that 350,000 working-people of Manchester and its environs live, almost all of them, in wretched, damp, filthy cottages, that the streets which surround them are usually in the most miserable and filthy condition, laid out without the slightest reference to ventilation, with reference solely to the profit secured by the contractor. In a word, we must confess that in the working-men's dwellings of Manchester, no cleanliness, no convenience, and consequently no comfortable family life is possible; that in such dwellings only a physically degenerate race, robbed of all humanity, degraded, reduced morally and physically to bestiality, could feel comfortable and at home.

Engels, 'Condition of the Working Class in England' (1845)

The materialist conception of history starts from the proposition that the production of the means to support human life and, next to production, the exchange of things produced, is the basis of all social structure; that in every society that has appeared in history, the manner in which wealth is distributed and society divided into classes or orders is dependent upon what is produced, how it is produced, and how the products are exchanged. From this point of view, the final causes of all social changes and political revolutions are to be sought, not in men's brains, not in men's better insights into eternal truth and justice, but in changes in the modes of production and exchange.

Engels, 'Socialism: Utopian & Scientific' (1880)

This sketch of the course of my studies in the domain of political economy is intended merely to show that my views – no matter how they may be judged and how little they conform to the interested prejudices of the ruling classes – are the outcome of conscientious research carried on over many years. At the entrance to science, as at the entrance to hell, the demand must be made:

> *Here must all hesitation be left behind.*
>
> *Here every cowardice must be no more.*

> (Dante, *The Divine Comedy*)

Marx, 'Preface' to *A Contribution to the Critique of Political Economy* (1859)

It was Marx who had first discovered the great law of motion of history, the law according to which all historical struggles, whether they proceed in the political, religious, philosophical or some other ideological domain, are in fact only the more or less clear expression of struggles of social classes, and that the existence and thereby the collisions, too, between these classes are in turn conditioned by the degree of development of their economic position, by the mode of their production and of their exchange determined by it. This law, which has the same significance for history as the law of the transformation of energy has for natural science.

Engels, 'Preface' to *The Eighteenth Brumaire of Louis Bonaparte* (1885)

In buying the labouring power of the workman, and paying its value, the capitalist, like every other purchaser, has acquired the right to consume or use the commodity bought ... the capitalist has acquired the right of using that labouring power during the *whole day or week*. He will, therefore, make him work daily, say, *twelve* hours. *Over and above* the six hours required to replace his wages, or the value of his labouring power, he will, therefore, have to work *six other hours*, which I shall call hours of *surplus-labour*, which surplus labour will realise itself in a *surplus-value* and a *surplus-produce*.

Marx, 'Value, Price and Profit' (1865; first published 1898)

It is *this sort of exchange between capital and labour* upon which capitalistic production, or the wages system, is founded, and which must constantly result in reproducing the working man as a working man, and the capitalist as a capitalist.

The rate of surplus-value, all other circumstances remaining the same, will depend on the proportion between that part of the working day necessary to reproduce the value of the labouring power and the *surplus-time* or *surplus-labour* performed for the capitalist. It will, therefore, depend on the *ratio in which the working day is prolonged over and above that extent*, by working which the working man would only reproduce the value of his labouring power, or replace his wages.

Marx, 'Value, Price and Profit' (1865; first published 1898)

…circumstances make men just as much as men make circumstances.

Marx & Engels, 'German Ideology' (1845-6; first published 1932)

The philosophers have only *interpreted* the world, in various ways; the point is to *change* it.

Marx, 'Theses on Feuerbach: Thesis XI' (1845; first published 1888)

Money is not a thing, it is a social relation.

Marx, 'Poverty of Philosophy' (1847)

But not only has the bourgeoisie forged the weapons that bring death to itself; it has also called into existence the men who are to wield those weapons – the modern working class – the proletarians.

Marx & Engels, 'Communist Manifesto' (1848)

As the economists are the scientific representatives of the bourgeois class, so the socialists and communists are the theorists of the proletarian class.

Marx, 'Poverty of Philosophy' (1847)

Profit rises to the extent that wages fall; it falls to the extent that wages rise.

Marx, 'Wage Labour and Capital' (1847; first published 1849)

Do not be deluded by the abstract word Liberty! Whose Liberty? Not the liberty of one individual in relation to another, but the liberty of Capital to crush the worker.

Marx, 'Speech on Free Trade' (1848)

All fixed, fast frozen relations, with their train of ancient and venerable prejudices and opinions, are swept away, all new-formed ones become antiquated before they can ossify. All that is solid melts into air, all that is holy is profaned...

Marx & Engels, 'Communist Manifesto' (1848)

Hegel remarks somewhere that all the great events and characters of world history occur, so to speak, twice. He forgot to add: the first time as *tragedy*, the second time as *farce*.

Marx, 'The Eighteenth Brumaire of Louis Bonaparte' (1852)

Competition generally, this essential locomotive force of the bourgeois economy, does not establish its laws, but is rather their executor. Unlimited competition is therefore not the presupposition for the truth of the economic laws, but rather the consequence – the form of appearance in which their necessity realises itself ... Competition therefore does not *explain* these laws; rather, it allows them be *seen*, but does not produce them.

Marx, 'Grundrisse' (1857; first published 1939)

The Communists disdain to conceal their opinions and ends. They openly declare that these ends can be attained only by the overthrow of all hitherto existing social arrangements. Let the ruling classes tremble at a Communist Revolution. The Proletarians have nothing to lose in it save their chains. They will gain a World.

Marx & Engels, 'Communist Manifesto' (1848)

It is not the consciousness of men that determines their being, but, on the contrary, their social being that determines their consciousness.

Marx, 'Preface' to *A Contribution to the Critique of Political Economy* (1859)

All London toilets discharge their physical ordure into the Thames through an ingenious system of underground sewer pipes. In the same way, through a system of goose quills, the world metropolis daily spills all its social ordure into a big paper-made central sewer – *The Daily Telegraph.*

Marx, 'Herr Vogt' (1860)

In broad outline, the Asiatic, ancient, feudal and modern bourgeois modes of production may be designated as epochs marking progress in the economic development of society.

Marx, 'Preface' to *A Contribution to the Critique of Political Economy* (1859)

Yesterday I found the courage at last to study your mathematical manuscripts ... The thing is as clear as daylight, so that we cannot wonder enough at the way the mathematicians insist on mystifying it. But this comes from the one-sided way these gentlemen think. To put $dy/dx = 0/0$, firmly and point-blank, does not enter their skulls. And yet it is clear that dy/dx can only be the pure expression of a completed process if the last trace of the *quanta x* and *y* has disappeared, leaving the expression of the preceding process of their change without any quantity ... At last we see clearly what mathematicians have claimed for a long time, without being able to present rational grounds, that the differential-*quotient* is the original, the differentials *dx* and *dy* are derived: the derivation of the formulae demands that both so-called irrational factors stand at the same time on one side of the equation, and only if you put the equation back into this its first form $dy/dx = f'(x)$, as you can see, are you free of the irrationals and instead have their rational expression.

Engels, 'Letter to Marx' (1881; unknown first publication)

Not only can we manage very well without the interference of the capitalist class in the great industries of the country, but that their interference is becoming more and more a nuisance.

Engels, 'Social Classes - Necessary and Superfluous' (1881)

The individual *is* the *social being*.

Marx, 'Economic and Philosophic Manuscripts' (1844; first published 1932)

The history of the decline of primitive communities (it would be a mistake to place them all on the same level; as in geological formations, these historical forms contain a whole series of primary, secondary, tertiary types, etc.) has still to be written. All we have seen so far are some rather meagre outlines. But in any event the research has advanced far enough to establish that: (1) the vitality of primitive communities was incomparably greater than that of Semitic, Greek, Roman, etc. societies, and, *a fortiori*, that of modern capitalist societies; (2) the causes of their decline stem from economic facts which prevented them from passing a certain stage of development...

Engels, 'Letter to Vera Zasulich' (1881; first published 1924)

...defects are inevitable in the first phase of communist society as it is when it has just emerged after prolonged birth pangs from capitalist society.

Marx, 'Critique of the Gotha Programme' (1875; first published 1891)

The worker receives means of subsistence in exchange for his labour, but the capitalist receives in exchange for his means of subsistence labour, the productive activity of the worker, the creative power whereby the worker not only replaces what he consumes but gives to the accumulated labour a greater value than it previously possessed.

Marx, 'Wage Labour and Capital' (1847; first published 1849)

Dialectics constitutes the most important form of thinking for present-day natural science, for it alone offers the analogue for, and thereby the method of explaining, the evolutionary processes occurring in nature, inter-connections in general, and transitions from one field of investigation to another.

Engels, 'On Dialectics' (1878; first published 1925)

The idea that political acts, grand performances of state, are decisive in history is as old as written history itself, and is the main reason why so little material has been preserved for us in regard to the really progressive evolution of the peoples which has taken place quietly, in the background, behind these noisy scenes on the stage.

Engels, 'Anti-Dühring' (1877)

All previous historical movements were movements of minorities, or in the interests of minorities. The proletarian movement is the self-conscious, independent movement of the immense majority, in the interest of the immense majority.

Marx & Engels, 'Communist Manifesto' (1848)

...the word "communist" ... means the follower of a definite revolutionary party...

Marx & Engels, 'German Ideology' (1845-6; first published 1932)

Quotes

What we understand by the economic conditions which we regard as the determining basis of the history of society are the methods by which human beings in a given society produce their means of subsistence and exchange the products among themselves (in so far as division of labour exists). Thus the *entire technique* of production and transport is here included. According to our conception, this technique also determines the method of exchange and, further, the division of products...

Engels, 'Letter to Borgius' (1894; first published 1895)

Needless to say, man is not free to choose *his productive forces* – upon which his whole history is based – for every productive force is an acquired force, the product of previous activity. Thus the productive forces are the result of man's practical energy, but that energy is in turn circumscribed by the conditions in which man is placed by the productive forces already acquired, by the form of society which exists before him, which he does not create, which is the product of the preceding generation.

Marx, 'Letter to Annenkov' (1846; first published 1912)

The interference of the State power in social relations becomes superfluous in one sphere after another, and then ceases of itself. The government of persons is replaced by the administration of things and the direction of the processes of production. The State is not "abolished", it withers away.

Engels, 'Anti-Dühring' (1877)

Quotes

Freedom does not consist in any dreamt-of independence from natural laws, but in the knowledge of these laws, and in the possibility this gives of systematically making them work towards definite ends.

Engels, 'Anti-Dühring' (1877)

When Class distinctions will have finally disappeared, and production will have been concentrated in the hands of this Association, which comprises the whole nation, the public power will lose its political character. Political power in the exact sense of the word, being the organised power of one class, which enables it to oppress another.

Marx & Engels, 'Communist Manifesto' (1848)

The concrete is concrete because it is the concentration of many determinations, hence unity of the diverse.

Marx, 'Grundrisse' (1857; first published 1939)

That woman was the slave of man at the commencement of society is one of the most absurd notions that has come down to us from the Enlightenment of the eighteenth century.

Engels, 'Origin of the Family, Private Property and the State', (1884)

Price is the money-name of the labour realised in a commodity.

Marx, 'Capital, Volume I' (1867)

Labour cannot emancipate itself in the white skin where in the black it is branded.

Marx, 'Capital, Volume I' (1867)

The State is … a product of society at a certain stage of development; it is the admission that this society has become entangled in an insoluble contradiction with itself, that it has split into irreconcilable opposites which it is powerless to dispel. But in order that these opposites, classes with conflicting economic interests, might not consume themselves and society in fruitless struggle, it became necessary to have a power seemingly standing above society which would alleviate the conflict and keep it within the bounds of "order"; and this power, having arisen out of society but placing itself above it, and alienating itself more and more from it, is the State.

Engels, 'Origin of the Family, Private Property and the State', (1884)

On the level plain, simple mounds look like hills; and the imbecile flatness of the present bourgeoisie is to be measured by the altitude of its great intellects.

Marx, 'Capital, Volume I' (1867)

In place of the old bourgeois society, with its classes and class antagonisms, we shall have an association in which the free development of each is the condition for the free development of all.

Marx & Engels, 'Communist Manifesto' (1848)

But if, as has now come about, production in its capitalist form produces a far greater abundance of the means of existence and development than capitalist society can consume, because capitalist society keeps the great mass of the real producers artificially removed from the means of existence and development; if this society is forced, by the law of its own existence, continually to increase production already too great for it, and, therefore, periodically every ten years, reaches a point where it itself destroys a mass not only of products but of productive forces, what sense is there still left in the talk about the "struggle for existence?" The struggle for existence can then only consist in the producing class taking away the control of production and distribution from the class hitherto entrusted with it but now no longer capable of it; that, however, is the socialist revolution.

Engels, 'Letter to Lavrov' (1875; first published 1936)

Nature builds no machines, no locomotives, railways, electric telegraphs, self-acting mules, etc. These are products of human industry; natural material transformed into organs of the human will over nature, or of human participation in nature. They are *organs of the human brain, created by the human hand*; the power of knowledge, objectified.

Marx, 'Grundrisse' (1857; first published 1939)

Revolutions are the locomotives of history.

Marx, 'The Class Struggles in France' (1850)

Communism now no longer meant the concoction, by means of the imagination, of an ideal society as perfect as possible, but insight into the nature, the conditions and the consequent general aims of the struggle waged by the proletariat.

Engels, 'On the History of the Communist League' (1885)

Every individual capital forms, however, but an individualised fraction, a fraction endowed with individual life, as it were, of the aggregate social capital, just as every individual capitalist is but an individual element of the capitalist class.

Marx, published by Engels 'Capital Volume II' (1885)

The only war left for ... Germany to wage will be *a world war*, a world war, moreover *of an extent the violence hitherto unimagined.* Eight to ten million soldiers will be at each other's throats and in the process they will strip Europe barer than a swarm of locusts. The depredations of the Years' War compressed into three to four years and extended over the entire continent; famine, disease, the universal lapse into barbarism.

Engels, 'Introduction to Borkheim' (1887)

Take it easy.

Engels, his favourite motto (during "Confessions" with Marx's daughter, Jenny), (1868; unknown first publication)

The State, then, has not existed from eternity. There have been societies that managed without it, that had no idea of the State and State authority. At a certain stage of economic development, which was necessarily bound up with the split of society into classes, the state became a necessity owing to this split. We are not rapidly approaching a stage in the development of production at which the existence of these classes not only will have ceased to be necessary, but will become a positive hindrance to production. They will fall as inevitably as they arose at an earlier stage. Along with them the state will inevitably fall. Society, which will reorganise production on the basis of a free and equal association of the producers, will put the whole machinery of State where it will then belong: into the museum of antiquities, by the side of the spinning-wheel and the bronze axe.

Engels, 'Origin of the Family, Private Property and the State', (1884)

We have no compassion and we ask no compassion from you. When our turn comes, we shall not make excuses for the terror. But the royal terrorists, the terrorists by the grace of God and the law, are in practice brutal, disdainful, and mean, in theory cowardly, secretive, and deceitful, and in both respects disreputable.

Marx, Editorial in *Neue Rheinische Zeitung* (1849)

The executive of the modern State is but a committee for managing the common affairs of the whole bourgeoisie.

Marx & Engels, 'Communist Manifesto' (1848)

The economic facts, which have so far played no role or only a contemptible one in the writing of history, are, at least in the modern world, a decisive historical force; that they form the basis of the origination of the present-day class antagonisms; that these class antagonisms, in the countries where they have become fully developed, thanks to large-scale industry, hence especially in England, are in their turn the basis of the formation of political parties and of party struggles, and thus of all political history. Marx had not only arrived at the same view, but had already, in the *Deutsche-Französische Jahrbücher* (1844), generalized it to the effect that, speaking generally, it is not the state which conditions and regulates the civil society at all, but civil society which conditions and regulates the state, and, consequently, that policy and its history are to be explained from the economic relations and their development, and not vice versa.

Engels, 'On the History of the Communist League' (1885)

Communism deprives no man of the power to appropriate the products of society; all that it does is to deprive him of the power to subjugate the labour of others by means of such appropriation.

Marx & Engels, 'Communist Manifesto' (1848)

Machines were, it may be said, the weapon employed by the capitalist to quell the revolt of specialised labour.

Marx, 'Poverty of Philosophy' (1847)

The working class will substitute, in the course of its development, for the old civil society an association which will exclude classes and their antagonism, and there will no longer be political power, properly speaking, since political power is simply the official form of antagonism in civil society.

Marx, 'Poverty of Philosophy' (1847)

The great basic question of all philosophy, especially of more recent philosophy, is that concerning the relation of thinking and being ... The answers which the philosophers gave to this question split them into two great camps. Those who asserted the primacy of spirit to nature and, therefore, in the last instance, assumed world creation in some form or other — and among the philosophers, Hegel, for example, this creation often becomes still more intricate and impossible than in Christianity — comprised the camp of *idealism*. The others, who regarded nature as primary, belong to the various schools of *materialism*.

Engels, 'Ludwig Feuerbach & the End of Classical German Philosophy' (1886)

What is society, irrespective of its form? The product of man's interaction upon man.

Marx, 'Letter to Annenkov' (1846; first published 1912)

That which is willed happens but rarely; in the majority of instances the numerous desired ends cross and conflict with one another, or these ends themselves are from the outset incapable of realisation, or the means of attaining them are insufficient. Thus the conflicts of innumerable individual wills and individual actions in the domain of history produce a state of affairs entirely analogous to that prevailing in the realm of unconscious nature.

Engels, 'Ludwig Feuerbach & the End of Classical German Philosophy' (1886)

Just as the savage must wrestle with Nature to satisfy his wants, to maintain and reproduce life, so must civilised man, and he must do so in all social formations and under all possible modes of production. With his development this realm of physical necessity expands as a result of his wants; but, at the same time, the forces of production which satisfy these wants also increase. Freedom in this field can only consist in socialised man, the associated producers, rationally regulating their interchange with Nature, bringing it under their common control, instead of being ruled by it as by the blind forces of Nature; and achieving this with the least expenditure of energy and under conditions most favourable to, and worthy of, their human nature. But it nonetheless still remains a realm of necessity. Beyond it begins that development of human energy which is an end in itself, the true realm of freedom, which, however, can blossom forth only with this realm of necessity as its basis. The shortening of the working-day is its basic prerequisite.

Marx, published by Engels 'Capital, Volume III' (1894)

Political, juridical, philosophical, religious, literary artistic, etc., development is founded on economic development. But each of these also reacts upon the others and upon the economic conditions. This is not to say that the economic situation is the *cause* and that it *alone* is *active* while everything else is simply passive effect, but rather that there is a reciprocal action founded, *in the final analysis*, on economic necessity which invariably prevails.

Engels, 'Letter to Borgius' (1894; first published 1895)

Freedom consists in converting the State from an organ superimposed upon society into one completely subordinate to it...

Marx, 'Critique of the Gotha Programme' (1875; first published 1891)

...the theologians ... Every religion but their own is an invention of men, while their own religion is an emanation from God.

Marx, 'Poverty of Philosophy' (1847)

In bourgeois society, therefore, the past dominates the present; in communist society, the present dominates the past. In bourgeois society capital is independent and has individuality, while the living person is dependent and has no individuality.

Marx & Engels, 'Communist Manifesto' (1848)

Let us not, however, flatter ourselves overmuch on account of our human victories over nature … we are reminded that we by no means rule over nature like a conqueror over a foreign people, like someone standing outside nature – but that we, with flesh, blood and brain, belong to nature, and exist in its midst, and that all our mastery of it consists in the fact that we have the advantage over all other creatures of being able to learn its laws and apply them correctly.

Engels, 'The Part Played by Labour in the Transition from Ape to Man' (1876; first published 1895-96)

The windmill gives you society with the feudal lord; the steam-mill, society with the industrial capitalist.

Marx, 'Poverty of Philosophy' (1847)

For we live not only in nature but also in human society, and this also has its evolution and its science no less than nature. It [is] therefore a question of bringing the science of society, that is, the sum total of the so-called historical and philosophical sciences, into harmony with the materialist foundation, and of reconstructing it thereupon.

Engels, 'Ludwig Feuerbach & the End of Classical German Philosophy' (1886)

To regard society as one single subject is, furthermore, to look at it wrongly; speculatively.

Marx, 'Grundrisse' (1857; first published 1939)

Individuals producing in society – hence socially determined individual production – is, of course, the point of departure.

Marx, 'Grundrisse' (1857; first published 1939)

Labour is the source of all wealth, the political economists assert. And it really is the source — next to nature, which supplies it with the material that it converts into wealth. But it is even infinitely more than this. It is the prime basic condition for all human existence, and this to such an extent that, in a sense, we have to say that *labour created man himself.*

Engels, 'The Part Played by Labour in the Transition from Ape to Man' (1876; first published 1895-96)

…it is not so much the particular political institutions of a country as the fundamental conditions of modern *bourgeois* society in general, which produce an average amount of crime in a given national fraction of society.

Marx, 'Capital Punishment' article in the *New-York Daily Tribune* (1853)

The division of labour reduces the worker to a degrading function; to this degrading function corresponds a depraved mind; with the depravity of mind goes a constant reduction of wages.

Marx, 'Poverty of Philosophy' (1847)

...according to the materialist conception of history, the determining factor in history is, *in the final analysis*, the production and reproduction of actual life. More than this was never maintained by either Marx or myself. Now if a person distorts this by declaring the economic to be the *only* determining factor, he changes that proposition into a meaningless, abstract, ridiculous piece of jargon. The economic conditions are the basis, but the various factors of the superstructure ... also have a bearing on the course of the historical struggles of which, in many cases, they largely determine the *form*.

Engels, 'Letter to Bloch' (1890; first published 1895)

Labour is the living, form-giving fire; it is the transitoriness of things, their temporality, as their formation by living time.

Marx, 'Grundrisse' (1857; first published 1939)

The division of society into a small, excessively rich class and a large, propertyless class of wage-workers results in a society suffocating from its own superfluity, while the great majority of its members is scarcely, or even at all, protected from extreme want. This state of affairs becomes daily more absurd and – more unnecessary. It *must* be abolished, it *can* be abolished.

Engels, 'Introduction' to *Wage Labour and Capital* (1891)

...with the abolition of class distinctions all social and political inequality arising from them would disappear of itself.

Marx, 'Critique of the Gotha Programme' (1875; first published 1891)

Labour being itself a commodity, measures itself as such by the labour-time necessary to produce this labour-commodity.

Marx, 'Poverty of Philosophy' (1847)

The country that is more developed industrially only shows, to the less developed, the image of its own future.

Marx, 'Preface' to the first German edition of *Capital, Vol. I* (1867)

Capital is the all-dominating economic power of bourgeois society. It must form the point of departure as well as the end-point.

Marx, 'Grundrisse' (1857; first published 1939)

What is known as 'Marxism' in France is, indeed, an altogether peculiar product — so much so that Marx once said to Lafargue: '*If anything is certain, it is that I myself am not a Marxist.*'

Engels, 'Letter to Eduard Bernstein' (1882; first published 1924)

A new social order is possible in which the present class differences will have disappeared and in which – perhaps after a short transitional period involving some privation, but at any rate of great value morally – through the planned utilisation and extension of the already existing enormous productive forces of all members of society, and with uniform obligation to work, the means for existence, for enjoying life, for the development and employment of all bodily and mental faculties will be available in an equal measure and in ever-increasing fullness.

Engels, 'Introduction' to *Wage Labour and Capital* (1891)

Everyone who knows anything of history also knows that great social revolutions are impossible without the feminine ferment. Social progress may be measured precisely by the social position of the fair sex...

Marx, 'Letter to Kugelmann' (1868; first published 1901-02)

The day when we are in the majority ... Yes, whatever the frightened bourgeois say, we are able to calculate the moment when we shall have the majority of the people behind us; our ideas are making headway everywhere, as much among teachers, doctors, lawyers, etc. as among the workers. If we had to start wielding power tomorrow, we should need engineers, chemists, agronomists. Well, it is my conviction that we would have a good many of them behind us already. In five or ten years we shall have more of them than we need.

Engels, 'Interview with *Le Figaro*' (1893)

I simply cannot understand how anyone can be envious of genius; it's something so very special that we who have not got it know it to be unattainable right from the start; but to be envious of anything like that one must have to be frightfully small-minded.

Engels, 'Letter to Bernstein' (1881; unknown first publication)

Only sound common sense, respectable fellow that he is, in the homely realm of his own four walls, has very wonderful adventures directly he ventures out into the wide world of research.

Engels, 'Anti-Dühring' (1877)

...human life has since time immemorial rested on production, and, in one way or another, on *social* production, whose relations we call, precisely, economic relations.

Marx, 'Grundrisse' (1857; first published 1939)

...*all* past history was the history of class struggles; that these warring classes of society are always the products of the modes of production and of exchange.

Engels, 'Anti-Dühring' (1877)

There is no royal road to science, and only those who do not dread the fatiguing climb of its steep paths have a chance of gaining its luminous summits.

Marx, 'Preface' to the first French edition of *Capital, Vol. I* (1872)

It is precisely *the alteration of nature* by men, not solely nature as such, which is the most essential and immediate basis of human thought.

Engels, 'Dialectics of Nature' (1883; first published 1925)

Nothing exists outside nature and man, and the higher beings our religious fantasies have created are only the fantastic reflection of our own essence.

Engels, 'Ludwig Feuerbach & the End of Classical German Philosophy' (1886)

Centralisation of the means of production and socialisation of labour at last reach a point where they become incompatible with their capitalist integument. Thus integument is burst asunder. The knell of capitalist private property sounds. The expropriators are expropriated.

Marx, 'Capital, Volume I' (1867)

...the question of what are known as great men. The fact that such and such a man, and he alone, should arise at a particular time in any given country, is, of course, purely fortuitous. But if we eliminate him, a replacement will be called for and such a replacement will be found – for better or for worse, but found he will ultimately be.

Engels, 'Letter to Borgius' (1894; first published 1895)

The bourgeois relations of production are the last antagonistic form of the social process of production – antagonistic not in the sense of individual antagonism but of an antagonism that emanates from the individuals' social conditions of existence – but the productive forces developing within bourgeois society create also the material conditions for a solution of this antagonism. The prehistory of human society accordingly closes with this social formation.

Marx, 'Preface' to *A Contribution to the Critique of Political Economy* (1859)

Both for the production on a mass scale of this communist consciousness, and for the success of the cause itself, the alteration of men on a mass scale is, necessary, an alteration which can only take place in a practical movement, a *revolution*; this revolution is necessary, therefore, not only because the *ruling* class cannot be overthrown in any other way, but also because the class *overthrowing* it can only in a revolution succeed in ridding itself of all the muck of ages and become fitted to found society anew.

Marx & Engels, 'German Ideology' (1845-6; first published 1932)

Only in community [with others has each] individual the means of cultivating his gifts in all directions; only in the community, therefore, is personal freedom possible.

Marx & Engels, 'German Ideology' (1845-6; first published 1932)

The general conclusion at which I arrived and which, once reached, became the guiding principle of my studies can be summarised as follows. In the social production of their existence, men inevitably enter into definite relations, which are independent of their will, namely relations of production appropriate to a given stage in the development of their material forces of production. The totality of these relations of production constitutes the economic structure of society, the real foundation, on which arises a legal and political superstructure and to which correspond definite forms of social consciousness. The mode of production of material life conditions the social, political and intellectual life process in general.

Marx, 'Preface' to *A Contribution to the Critique of Political Economy* (1859)

And here it becomes evident, that the bourgeoisie is unfit any longer to be the ruling class in society, and to impose its conditions of existence upon society as an over-riding law. It is unfit to rule because it I incompetent to assure an existence to its slave within his slavery, because it cannot help letting him sink into such a state, that it has to feed him, instead of being fed by him. Society can no longer live under this bourgeoisie, in other words, its existence is no longer compatible with society.

Marx & Engels, 'Communist Manifesto' (1848)

The right of the landowners can be traced back to robbery.

Marx, 'Economic and Philosophic Manuscripts' (1844; first published 1932)

All science would be superfluous if the outward appearance and the essence of things directly coincided.

Marx, published by Engels 'Capital, Volume III' (1894)

In the crises of the world market, the contradictions and antagonisms of bourgeois production are strikingly revealed. Instead of investigating the nature of the conflicting elements which erupt in the catastrophe, the apologists content themselves with denying the catastrophe itself and insisting, in the face of their regular and periodic recurrence, that if production were carried on according to the textbooks, crises would never occur.

Marx, 'Theories of Surplus Value, Book Two' (1862; first published 1905-10)

Violence is the midwife of every old society that is pregnant with a new one.

Marx, 'Capital, Volume I' (1867)

In all forms of society there is one specific kind of production which predominates over the rest ... a general illumination which bathes all the other colours and modifies their particularity.

Marx, 'Grundrisse' (1857; first published 1939)

Just as Darwin discovered the law of development or organic nature, so Marx discovered the law of development of human history: the simple fact, hitherto concealed by an overgrowth of ideology, that mankind must first of all eat, drink, have shelter and clothing, before it can pursue politics, science, art, religion, etc.; that therefore the production of the immediate material means, and consequently the degree of economic development attained by a given people or during a given epoch, form the foundation upon which the state institutions, the legal conceptions, art, and even the ideas on religion, of the people concerned have been evolved, and in the light of which they must, therefore, be explained, instead of vice versa, as had hitherto been the case.

Engels, 'Speech at the Graveside of Karl Marx' (1883)

[The working class] have no ready-made utopias to introduce *by decree of the people*. They know that in order to work out their own emancipation, and along with it that higher form to which present society is irresistibly tending by its own economic agencies, they will have to pass through long struggles, through a series of historical processes, transforming circumstances and men. They have no ideals to realise, but to set free elements of the new society with which old collapsing bourgeois society itself is pregnant.

Marx, 'The Civil War in France' (1871)

Nothing human is alien to me.

Marx, his favourite maxim (during "Confessions" with relatives), (1865; unknown first publication)

The sun is now shining, so the moment for going for a walk has come …

Marx, 'Letter to Engels' (1882; unknown first publication)

Now as for myself, I do not claim to have discovered either the existence of classes in modern society or the struggle between them … My own contribution was 1. To show that the *existence of classes* is merely bound up with *particular historical phases in the development of production*; 2. that the class struggle necessarily leads to the *dictatorship of the proletariat*; 3. that this dictatorship itself only constitutes no more than a transition to the *abolition of all classes* and to *a classless society.*

Marx, 'Letter to Weydemeyer' (1852; first published 1930)

My inquiry led me to the conclusion that neither legal relations nor political forms could be comprehended whether by themselves or on the basis of a so-called general development of the human mind, but on the contrary they originate in the material conditions of life … that the anatomy of this civil society, however, has to be sought in political economy.

Marx, 'Preface' to *A Contribution to the Critique of Political Economy* (1859)

There are many females in the world, and some among them are beautiful. But where could I find again a face, whose every feature, even every wrinkle, is a reminder of the greatest and sweetest memories of my life? Even my endless pains, my irreplaceable losses I read in your sweet countenance, and I kiss away the pain when I kiss your sweet face...

Marx, 'Love letter to his wife Jenny' (1865; unknown first publication)

On the 14th of March, at a quarter to three in the afternoon, the greatest living thinker ceased to think. He had been left alone for scarcely two minutes, and when we came back we found him in his armchair, peacefully gone to sleep – but forever.

Engels, 'Speech at the Grave of Karl Marx' (1883)

I arrived at my conclusions through an entirely empirical analysis based on an exhaustive critical study of political economy.

Marx, 'Economic and Philosophic Manuscripts' (1844; first published 1932)

His name will endure through the ages, and so also will his work.

Engels, 'Speech at the Grave of Karl Marx' (1883)

A Select Bibliography of Works by Marx and Engels:

Marx, 1843, *On the Jewish Question*

Marx, 1843-4, *A Contribution to the Critique of Hegel's Philosophy of Right. Introduction.*

Engels, 1844, *Outlines of a Critique of Political Economy*

Marx, 1844, *Economic and Philosophical Manuscripts*

Engels, 1845, *Condition of the Working Class in England*

Marx & Engels, 1845, *The Holy Family*

Marx, 1845, *Theses on Feuerbach*

Marx & Engels, 1845-6, *The German Ideology*

Marx, 1846-7, *The Poverty of Philosophy*

Marx, 1847, *Wage-Labour and Capital*

Marx & Engels, 1848, *Manifesto of the Communist Party*

Marx, 1850, *The Class Struggles in France, 1848-1850*

Marx, 1852, *The Eighteenth Brumaire of Louis Bonaparte*

Marx & Engels, 1852-61, Articles in the *New York Daily Tribune*

Marx, 1857-8, *Grundrisse*

Marx, 1859, *A Contribution to the Critique of Political Economy*

Marx, 1861-3, *Theories of Surplus Value* (Vol. 1-3)

Marx, 1864, *Inaugural Address of the International Working Men's Association*

Marx, 1865, *Value, Price and Profit*

Marx, 1867, *Capital*, Vol. I

Marx, 1871, *The Civil War in France*

Marx, 1875, *Critique of the Gotha Programme*

Engels, 1876-8, *Anti-Duhring*

Engels, 1880, *Socialism: Utopian and Scientific*

Engels, 1873-83, *Dialectics of Nature*

Engels, 1884, *The Origin of the Family, Private Property and the State*

Marx, 1885, *Capital*, Vol. II

Engels, 1886, *Ludwig Feuerbach and the End of Classical German Philosophy*

Marx, 1894, *Capital*, Vol. III

Suggested Further Reading: The following editions of works by Marx and Engels are useful points of entry into the study of their thought. These publications are especially recommend because of the highly useful introductions/forewords they present.

Karl Marx, *Early Writings*, Penguin Classics edition, 1992 (introduced by Lucio Colletti)

Karl Marx, *Political Writings* in 3 Volumes, Penguin Classics edition, 1992 (introduced by David Fernbach)

Karl Marx, *Grundrisse*, Penguin Classics edition, 1993 (Foreword by Martin Nicolaus)

Marx & Engels, *The German Ideology*, Student Edition, Lawrence & Wishart, 1970 (introduced by C.J. Arthur)

Karl Marx, *Capital*, in 3 Volumes, Penguin Classics Edition, 1990 (introduced by Ernest Mandel)

Marx & Engels, *Selected Works*, one-volume edition, Lawrence & Wishart, 1968

A Note on the Source Texts

An excellent archival source for the collected writings of Marx and Engels is the State Socio-Political Library, Moscow (the library of the former Institute of Marxism-Leninism). Its vast archives are accessible to researchers. Another is the International Institute of Social History in Amsterdam. Both institutions are – together with a number of others – involved with the *Gesamtausgabe* project, for the eventual publication of Marx and Engels' complete works (in 120 volumes).

The quotes appearing in this book are derived from already in-print materials. I have cited the year of first publication for all quoted sources, aside from a small number where I have been unable to ascertain details of initial publication (and I am happy to make any necessary changes / acknowledgements to future editions of this publication). Under UK and US law, copyright typically expires 70 years after the death of the author; and pre-1923 publications are in the public domain. As stated above, many of Marx and Engels' writings (e.g. *Capital*, and the letters and articles in *Deutsch-Französische Jahrbücher*) were published during their own lifetime (Marx died in 1883, Engels died in 1895), and such copyright expired long ago. A number of their works were only published after 1923. Of these, many (e.g. *The German Ideology* and *Economic and Philosophic Manuscripts of 1844*) were published for the first time by David Riazanov (1870-1938), as director of the Marx-Engels Institute, which he founded in 1919 (with many works undertaken by Progress Publishers, a now defunct Soviet publisher). Another such important text, published after 1923, is the *Grundrisse* (published in full for the first time in 1939-41; although Kautsky had earlier published its 'Introduction', in 1903).

Over 70 years have elapsed since the initial publication of such works as *The German Ideology* and *Grundrisse*. These publications do themselves represent derivative works of Marx and Engels' writings, (presenting editorial revisions, translations, annotations, elaborations, and other modifications of the hitherto unpublished manuscripts). The copyright of these first publications is thus expired, and all such works are now in the public domain (although newer translations retain copyright). It is here taken that use of these older texts, first published over 70 years ago – presenting them, and deriving new English adaptations from them – is Fair Use.

Printed in Great Britain
by Amazon